CROCODILE

EVOLUTION'S GREATEST SURVIVOR
CROCODILE

LYNNE KELLY

ALLEN&UNWIN

First published in 2006

Allen & Unwin
83 Alexander Street
Crows Nest NSW 2065
Australia
Phone: (61 2) 8425 0100
Fax: (61 2) 9906 2218
Email: info@allenandunwin.com
Web: www.allenandunwin.com

National Library of Australia
Cataloguing-in-Publication entry:

Kelly, Lynne.
Crocodile: evolution's greatest survivor.
Bibliography.
Includes index.
ISBN 978 1 74114 498 7.

1. Crocodilians. I. Title.

597.98

Internal design by Lisa White
Maps by Ian Faulkner
Illustrations on pp. 1, 21 and 101 by Lisa White, and all other illustrations by Ian Faulkner
Set in 11.5/17 pt Adobe Garamond by Midland Typesetters, Australia
Printed in Australia by Ligare Book Printer, Sydney

10 9 8 7 6 5 4 3 2 1

For Damian

CONTENTS

ACKNOWLEDGEMENTS

There have been many people who have been greatly valued during the writing of this book. Librarians at the State Library of Victoria, the Yarra Plenty Regional Library Service (especially the guys on the mobile), and the various branches of the Library of the University of Melbourne will be forever in my debt. I did not encounter a single one who was not keen to help, despite many obscure and vague requests.

Crocodilian experts are a rare breed, obsessive about their chosen creatures. Dr Steven Salisbury, of the University of Queensland, could not have been more helpful. As an authority on fossil crocodilians, he offered much expert advice on this complex area. He was also very encouraging, and the books and articles he recommended were invaluable.

Dr Adam Britton maintains the wonderful website, www.crocodilian.com, which is the best reference (online or otherwise) on the biology of living species. Adam was extremely accommodating and enthusiastic, sharing his wealth of knowledge and experience freely. I greatly appreciate his checking relevant sections of my work for accuracy. Any remaining mistakes are entirely mine.

I gratefully acknowledge the time, expertise and food of John and Lillian Lever and the staff at the Koorana Crocodile Farm, Queensland. Jon Birkett of the Royal Melbourne Zoological Gardens, Greg Parker of the Ballarat Wildlife Park and Elizabeth O'Callaghan of the Warrnambool and District Historical Society were also most helpful. The writings of Grahame Webb, Charlie Manolis and Deborah Cadbury were thoroughly enjoyed while they provided much needed information and inspiration. In Charles A. Ross's excellent encyclopaedia, *Crocodiles and Alligators*, the writings of Hans-Dieter Sues, Eric Buffetaut and G.W. Trompf were particularly valuable.

At Allen & Unwin, I would very much like to thank Ian Bowring for asking me to write this book and then offering advice and encouragement throughout the process. I would also like to thank Catherine Taylor for her excellent editorial skills.

At a personal level, I would like to thank my husband, Damian Kelly, for his unswerving support and for sharing every step in the development of this book. The support of those close to me is indispensable. In particular, I would like to thank Edna King-Smith, Rebecca and Rudi Heitbaum, Peter King-Smith, Tony King-Smith, Val and John Jacobson, Lisa Jacobson, Sue King-Smith, Ian Irvine, David Curzon, Jenny and Sam Ginsberg and Ian Rowland. Without family and friends like these, life would be very much the poorer.

I revel in the knowledge that a book will survive long into the future, when those now too young to read it may open its pages. This is constantly brought home to me by the treasured presence of Abigail and Leah Heitbaum.

INTRODUCTION

Few animals inspire the sort of awe and fear that the crocodilians do. Those who share their habitats tread warily at the water's edge, and their mythology abounds with stories and legends of these giant predators. The more dangerous the species, the more fearsome the tales of its exploits, but these tales have arisen from actual observations of the real animal.

Fossilised remains of crocodilian ancestors dating back over two hundred million years have been found, their resemblance to their modern counterparts unmistakable. The word 'crocodile' comes from the Greek word, *krokodeilos*, meaning lizard. The Greek historian Herodotus used the term 'crocodrilos'. In Greek, 'kroke' means 'pebble' and 'drilos' means 'worm', so Herodotus may have marvelled at the giant Nile crocodiles basking on the pebbled shores of the river and named them accordingly.

The term 'crocodilian' covers three different families of animals—the 'true' crocodiles, the alligators and the gharials. There are fourteen species of true crocodiles, all of whom live in tropical climates. The term 'crocodile' is commonly used to cover all three families and all members of their ancient ancestral line. Zoologists use the term 'true crocodile' to distinguish the modern crocodile family, *Crocodylidae.* The Australian freshwater crocodile is one of the smaller, relatively harmless members of this family. The massive 'saltie', the saltwater crocodile, is the family's largest and most aggressive member. There are eight species of alligators, six of whom are classed as caimans, that live in cooler climes and there is the Indian branch of the crocodilian family, the gharial.

Alligators and crocodiles have much in common, but the most obvious differences are in their jaws. All crocodilians have powerful jaws that can exert many times the pressure of the most powerful canine jaws. But whereas crocodiles have elongated jaws that taper almost to a point, alligators have thicker, more rounded jaws, ideally suited for crushing the hard shells of one of their preferred foods, turtles. Crocodiles eat a huge variety of prey but, in general, the narrower the jaw, the more likely it is that fish is the mainstay of their diet. Crocodiles are also distinguished by their prominent fourth tooth which remains visible when the jaws are closed. Of course, every rule has its exception. The Indian mugger, classified as a crocodile, has a broad jaw.

The broad family groupings and family resemblances of the crocodilians have been established, but classification arguments still continue in the detail of species and subspecies, especially of the caimans. This is part of the fascination of the crocodile—naturalists want to classify them; palaeontologists want to investigate their links to the era of the dinosaurs; creationists want to deny their fossil record; hunters see them as the ultimate trophy; while conservationists are trying to halt the destruction of their surroundings and protect their dwindling numbers.

I have always loved natural history: animals, plants, classification and the way it all fits together. From the starting point of native mammals, to birds and then to spiders, I have obsessed about one animal or another for as long as I can remember. When my publisher suggested that I turn my attention to crocodiles, I was a little stunned. Here was an animal I had thought very little about. I admitted no expertise but expressed an enthusiasm to check them out. Very soon I realised I had been set the challenge to write about one of the most intriguing animals on the planet. How could I have gone so long and not known this stuff? People have loved them, hated them, feared them, revered them, studied them obsessively and written all sorts of myths around them. I had all that wonderful literature to explore.

Whatever the reason for the fascination crocodiles, alligators, caimans and gharials hold for humans, I hope that the stories I have included here will show you that the relationship is never dull.

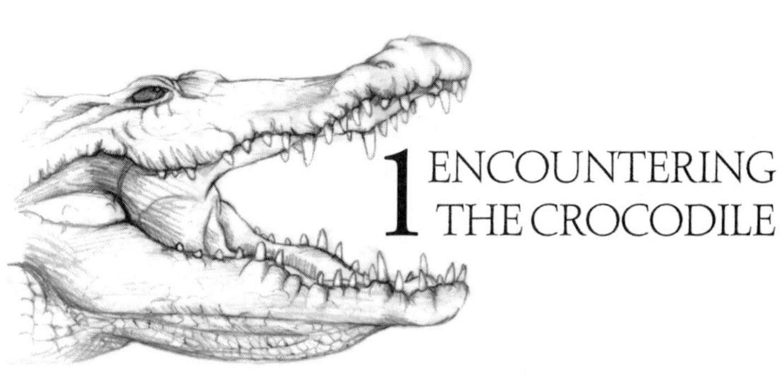

1 ENCOUNTERING THE CROCODILE

When the world was still young Gumangan, the crocodile-man, and Birik-birik, the plover-man, were always together. They owned a set of fire sticks which they used to make fire. When Gumangan returned from hunting one day, he found Birik-birik asleep, with no fire ready for cooking the food. In anger, Gumangan grabbed the fire sticks, intending to take them to the river where he would dip them in the water so they would never make fire again. But Birik-birik was not beaten. He got the sticks back from Gumangan and ran into the hills, thus preserving the valuable fire forever. Their friendship over, the crocodile always lives near the water and the plover lives in the hills.

The nineteenth century was a time in which explorers set off around the world collecting exotic animals in their thousands. I found it inspiring to read of familiar creatures through the eyes of one young sailor on the famous British survey sloop, the *Beagle*. In a personal journal, not written for dramatic effect but merely as a private record, the excitement of Helpman seeing the saltwater crocodile for the first time in its natural habitat was infectious. As the small party explored the now well-known Victoria and Adelaide rivers in Australia's far north, the sight of the huge populations of crocodiles in that setting was so overwhelming that he referred to the scene as 'magnificent' and that day as 'perhaps the happiest in my life'.

Those who set off on voyages of exploration and surveying in the nineteenth century did so in the knowledge that they would not see their homeland or their loved ones for years, if, indeed, they returned at all. The unlucky ones might founder on a reef or run foul of the 'savages' who inhabited the lands they were exploring, but the lucky ones would survive to tell tales of strange new lands and the exotic flora and fauna that lived there.

Benjamin Francis Helpman was one of the lucky ones. At the age of twenty-three, in 1837, he took up his commission as Master's Mate on HMS Survey Sloop *Beagle*. The little ship made famous by Charles Darwin on its previous voyag e from 1831 to 1936 was being prepared for her third round-the-world voyage, her second to Australia.

Portrait of Benjamin Francis Helpman by G.L. Marchant. (Reproduced with permission from the State Library of Victoria)

Born in Devonshire on 20 December 1814, Helpman was one of seven children. The four boys in the family all entered the navy. Helpman served in the West Indies and Lisbon, and on at least four vessels, before taking the commission on the *Beagle*, although little else is known of his life prior to him writing his journals. It is thanks to these journals, faithfully kept throughout his travels, that we can see the wonders Helpman saw through his eyes, one such wonder being the creature he called an 'Alligator'.

The aim of the voyage was to survey the hitherto unexplored great northern rivers of the southern continent. Helpman's understandable excitement at being part of such an enormous undertaking was tempered by his sorrow at leaving his home and loved ones so far behind him. By the time of sailing,

Helpman's father had died, but he remained very close to his mother and sisters. And he was leaving behind the young woman he adored, his beloved Sarah.

Conditions on board the *Beagle* were so cramped that Helpman had only four pocket handbooks in which to record the experiences of many months. Making his own ink, he wrote in such tiny script that his transcriber, E.M. Christie, had to use a magnifying glass to decipher each word. The length of the voyage and monotony of life at sea meant that Helpman had lost some of his enthusiasm for the venture by the time he caught his first glance of New Holland, in November 1837. 'I had the pleasure of seeing the first of New Holland, 'twas Rottnest Island . . . A barren, sterile, beastly place . . . I have lost a great deal of my roaming notions. I would not have Sarah see such a Country, with the idea of living in it, for anything.'

Helpman had been bitterly disappointed when the *Beagle* arrived at the Cape of Good Hope to find there were no letters from Sarah waiting for him. Nonetheless, Helpman's youth meant that times of very low spirits were countered by his very real elation at the job ahead: '100 miles more—Hurrah! And then we shall be at places never yet seen by Europeans!!! What pleasure! An unbeaten path—something to learn and do that never was yet seen or done.'

Having landed and revictualled at Fremantle, in Western Australia, the *Beagle* headed north. The first great river to be named was the Fitzroy, in honour of the *Beagle*'s captain on her previous voyage. It was here that Helpman first mentioned

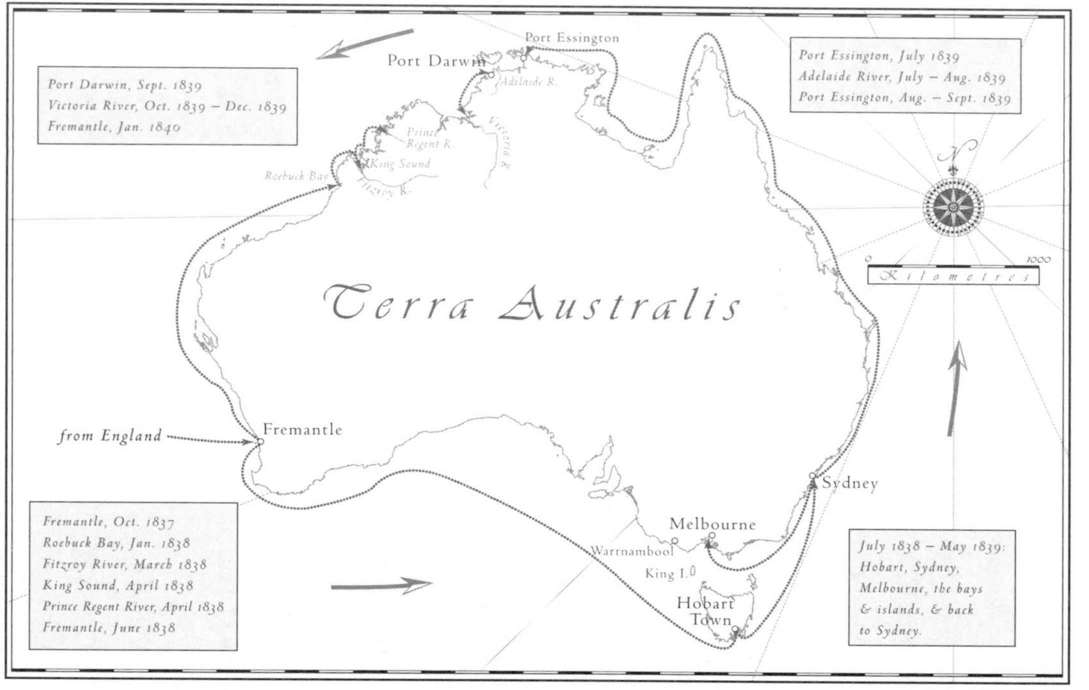

Benjamin Francis Helpman's voyage on the HMS Survey Sloop Beegle, *1837–40.*

the 'Alligator'. 'Weeks found the upper half of the head of an Alligator, I fancy about 2 feet long, it was quite bleached.' Helpman's 'Alligator' was the estuarine or saltwater crocodile, *Crocodylus porosus.* Widespread throughout the tropics, the saltwater crocodile has a range of local names but in Australia it is affectionately known as the 'saltie'.

Sailors in those days often took to watching wildlife and became keen naturalists. Helpman was no exception. As the *Beagle* continued on its winding route along the coast and into the waterways of the north-west, Helpman describes turtles, whales, sea snakes and sharks, along with the continual nuisance of mosquitoes and sandflies. He describes learning to fish with members of the local indigenous tribes, whose skills he greatly admired. He collected shells and observed myriad new species of birds, many of whom were shot for food or as specimens. As they explored further inland, Helpman wrote: 'There was a Rat of immense size, who would not move for the poke of a stick.' He says of the islands in Westernport: 'These islands are a complete store for Birds, Beasts, and Fishes. There are Kangaroo, Wallaby, Opossum, Squirrel and Flying Squirrel, Kangaroo Rats and Mice. Swan, Black Duck, Curlew, Oyster Birds, Storks and innumerable others—Fish of all kinds.'

Two years after leaving England, the *Beagle* began to map the unexplored coastline of the far north of Australia—prime crocodile territory. At Plymouth Island, Helpman wrote: 'There are a very great number of Alligators here and they have been troublesome, one has been shot, after it had carried off a Dog and a blanket, both of which were found in him.' Late in July 1839, the *Beagle* arrived at a pristine river environment, one of the best habitats for crocodiles in the world. Helpman recorded his first sighting of a crocodile in Adam Bay:

> As the Sun rose, flocks of Parakeets of splendid plumage were seen in all directions. In the afternoon saw an immense Alligator; the first [time] I have ever seen such a monster, went away to shoot it but missed it, firing over it.
>
> Ordered to prepare to go up the rivers tomorrow; Captain and Emery in the Gig, and I with the Whaler. This, I suppose, is a singular mark of his favour, at any rate 'tis just what I hoped would happen. A white frock and pair of trowsers, a tin pot, a plate and spoon—the very thought of going away to see anything new is pleasant—novelty—change—anything but rest for the mind.

Helpman might well record his alligator as being 'immense'. *Crocodylus porosus* is one of the largest of all the living crocodiles, with specimens being recorded at 6 metres in length and weighing over 1000 kilograms. The species name, *porosus*, comes from the Greek for 'callus', and bears witness to the calluses found on the snouts of saltwater crocodiles.

Travelling with the party in the smaller boat, Helpman continued noting his observations as the *Beagle* remained in the estuary of what would be named the Adelaide River.

*The snout of a saltwater crocodile (*Crocodylus porosus*) shows the calluses for which it was named. Also note the prominent tooth on the lower jaw which distinguishes crocodiles from alligators. (Courtesy Damian Kelly)*

Monday. July, 29th, 1839. At 4.0 a.m. started away, and exactly at sunrise reached the entrance of the opening, which we followed up. It gradually trended to the S.E., and, to our great delight found every appearance of a River, having deep water, 7 fathoms, the general breadth ½ a mile. With a flood tide, and being very anxious, we got an immense distance up, not less than 20 miles, when all doubts were at an end; we were now in a River, the largest and finest known in New Holland, it having a perfect ship entrance, with plenty of water to this point.

The River was here 300 yards wide. We landed at 10.0 a.m. to get breakfast and sights for Latitude and Longitude. The land is exceedingly level, and soil good, of fine rich mould. We remarked that each alternate reach was wooded on the opposite side, and immediately opposite was a clear open space. The reaches were very serpentine, the points rounded.

What Helpman is describing here is perfect crocodile country. The wide, deep river enables the crocodile to hunt with ease, stalking its prey and then lying in wait, almost invisible from the river bank. Crocodiles feed and hunt mainly in the water. They come up on to the river bank to sunbake, which helps them to maintain their body temperature, and they nest there in the breeding season. The saltwater crocodile particularly likes mangrove-lined tidal rivers. Helpman describes a tropical river rich with wildlife, offering easy pickings for the resident crocodiles.

> Whilst we were coming up, at about daylight, 6 fine Mullet jumped into the boats, which, with a fine large Catfish which was caught, gave us a sumptuous meal.
>
> We had now quite cleared the Mangroves, and the clumps of trees on each side were evident forest. The land had still the same appearance parched up, and there were several fires spreading in all directions. The numbers of Alligators' beds in the grass made it rather dangerous walking. We saw a great number, about 10 feet, floating with their heads just showing above the water; the eye being on the upper part they sink almost without motion, which is very singular.

Helpman is describing the typical swimming and lurking behaviour of not only the saltwater crocodile, but all crocodilians. Only the nostrils at the tip of the snout and the eyes, perched high on the head, break the surface of the water. The crocodile's ability to move almost soundlessly through the water, making scarcely a ripple on the surface, means that there is little to warn potential prey of its presence. The 'beds in the grass' are also typical of good saltwater crocodile country. During the wet season, from November to March, the female crocodiles build their mound nests from grass and mud.

> After dinner we again pushed on, still carrying deep water—7, 8 and 9 fathoms—general breadth 250 yards; the general length of each reach ¾ of a mile, and very serpentine indeed, rounding from S.E. by E. suddenly to S.W. The grassy plains commenced from about 14 miles up; occasionally mud banks from which the Alligators came sliding off. After getting our dinner we again shoved off, but did not get above 5 or 6 miles higher up when we came to, lashing the boats together, and as I had joined the Captain's and Emery's mess I found it quite pleasant . . .
>
> Thursday. July, 30th, 1839. At 4.0 weighed, and continued our winding progress; the River still maintaining its breadth, depth, and numbers of Alligators. As the day broke, the scene became magnificent, and I think it was about the happiest of my life . . .
>
> We landed for breakfast on a large plain of rich soil and thick grass, but still no appearance of any elevations.
>
> We were not very long at this meal, everyone feeling very anxious to push on. Immense flocks of Birds, Cockatoos, Ducks and Geese were now seen. The Ducks are very much

like Teal, only larger, and without any bright feathers. But the most singular part of the whole is, that both Ducks and Geese were perched on dead trees in immense flocks. We shot a number of Ducks, but the Geese were too shy. Ibis, in great quantities were now seen . . . The Alligators now became very thick, and one of them showed a great inclination to dispute my right to a duck, and did not give it up until we were close to it.

We landed about 11.0 for latitude. The Bamboo was now the principal thing seen, and we dined under them. They are really splendid, not above a few inches in diameter at the bottom they gradually taper to a fine hairbreadth at 60 or 70 feet high. We saw amongst the high grass, quantities of nests of Alligators, and the places where they had been basking in the sun. The land still open, and rich grassy plains, but each alternate reach wooded on the opposite side. It was here about 250 yards wide and 7 fathoms deep. After dinner we again pushed on, and in one of the reaches came on immense quantities of Vampires. When on the wing they look exactly like Crows, being much of that size. They were hanging by the hooks of their wings with their heads down, and the wings wrapped close around them. They were in clusters of thousands, and the noise they made was a scream, and they smell abominably. I was glad, after my curiosity had been satisfied at the expense of my olfactory nerves, to get off. The Thermometer was, during the day, 94, and at night, 66. Just as we were coming to for the night, we saw

> high land, and landed and found it an elevated ridge about 2 miles off, but not above 150 feet high. The entire features of the country unaltered, being still clear, open plains, and fine soil. The water was now quite fresh, and had been for some miles. I again had a very pleasant nap.

The temperature range Helpman describes here, from 19ºC to 36ºC, is perfect for the heat-loving crocodiles, and for the animals he calls 'Vampires', otherwise known as the black flying fox (*Pteropus alecto*) or Gould's fruit bat. These bats roost in colonies of hundreds of thousands and it is no surprise that such dense populations of crocodiles favour the same territory. The crocodile is capable of leaping high out of the water to reach prey, or even tail-walking in the way we are more used to seeing with dolphins. Fruit bats roosting in trees overhanging the river are easy pickings. Birds, fish and animals drinking at the water's edge offer a varied diet to the river's largest inhabitants.

On Wednesday 31 July 1839, Helpman wrote of fearing the harmless 'Vampires' while recording less fear of the animal which now has such a deadly reputation—his Alligators. Clearly, others in his crew were less relaxed about potentially fatal encounters.

> About 3.00 p.m. we came to a reach, about 1¼ miles long, thick wood on the banks, and to our astonishment found it completely filled with Vampires.

There must have been millions, they were frightened at us, and as they cannot fly, except from the top boughs, many broke down and came into the river, where numbers of Alligators were waiting to receive them. They were so thick as to completely darken the entire reach, and even when the trees appeared quite filled, nor do I think 'twould have been possible for them to have [all] been on the wing together. They are generally considered very dangerous, and if they had taken it into their heads, we could not have formed a mouthful for a thousandth part. What with their noise and smell, it was almost insufferable . . .

Whilst we were at this place, with both boats lashed together, an Alligator got in between us, but whether with the intention of getting into the boat or not I cannot guess; he made a terrible fuss when first seen, in getting away. The Mosquitoes were very troublesome, especially when the Captain and I landed at 10.0 p.m. for sights. The tracks of the Kangaroos were very plain, and at night we heard several come down to drink. In spite of every obstacle I slept soundly. Thermometer day 92, night 68 . . .

After the dinner, whilst the boat's crews were taking a siesta, two Alligators made attempts to get into the boats, and so frightened one of the men (Lobb) as not to be able to speak for some time.

After six days of surveying, Helpman and his small band returned to the *Beagle,* to the relief of the remaining crew, who had been worried that the explorers had been lost. They completed the surveys and named the river they had so admired the Adelaide River, in honour of Queen Adelaide, the widow of King William IV and the Dowager Queen of England. The Alligator river system was later named for its huge crocodile population, reflecting the common use of the term back then. These rivers lie 100 kilometres to the east of the Adelaide River, in what is now Kakadu National Park.

Leaving the Adelaide River, the *Beagle* sailed on westward to the young town of Port Darwin. Pressing further west beyond Port Darwin along the northernmost coast of Australia, the *Beagle* came to a huge river, which necessitated months of exploration to produce a detailed survey map. Storms and excessive heat, sandflies and mosquitoes, along with the constant search for fresh water, dominate Helpman's journal.

> It has not been named yet; I suppose the magnitude of it must first be known before the illustrious name it has to bear is known. At noon we entered the heads. It is about 1½ miles broad, the land on both sides high and almost barren. There are quite a few stunted trees which saves its credit, the points are all rocky, altogether it was a most miserable place. About 2.0 we had reached about 10 miles inside the Heads, Came to and moored. The Country is deeply cut up, quite loose stone. The low land appears to be all Mangroves, and covered at high water. The Thermometer altered after entering the Heads to 92 . . .

> The average heat during the day, under cover in a box was 104, and 101 in the breeze; during the calms the heat was almost insufferable, my hands and neck blistered. We were boarded by Mosquitoes, who gave us, fortunately, a short visit . . . On the Eastern side, singular high round flat-toped hills run as far as the eye can reach; as you alter the position they assume a fresh shape, sometimes very fantastical. Slept very soundly on the thwart, too warm to bear the clothes; rather a rough bed-place. Dined with a tin pot, a spoon and a plate. Everything novel, and all to see. Who would not be happy?

This river was the home of a saltwater crocodile whose skull now resides in the British Museum of Natural History and whose demise was recorded both by Helpman and the *Beagle*'s Captain, John Lort Stokes. Stokes's journals contain a lively account of the crocodile's death:

> *November 3*.—Starting early, we had just passed all the shoals in the neighbourhood of Curiosity Peak, and entered a narrow part of the river, when the leadsman in the bows of the boat reported, 'A large alligator coming downstream, sir.' Elated by the expectation of sport, we instantly grounded the boat on the right bank to keep her steady, and waited anxiously for the monster's approach. It will readily be believed, that every eye was fixed upon him as he slowly advanced, scarcely disturbing the glassy surface of the water, and quite unconscious of the fate that impended over him.

At length he came abreast, and about eighty yards off, only the flat crown of his head, and the partly serrated ridge along his back, appearing in sight. It was a moment of deep excitement for us all, and every one held his breath in suspense as I pointed my gun at the brute's head. I felt confident of hitting my mark; but judging from the little effect I had produced on former occasions, scarcely dreamt of the execution my ball actually did . . . I fired, and never heard a ball strike with more satisfaction in my life. It laid the alligator sprawling, feet uppermost. There was no time to be lost in getting him on shore; two or three strokes with the oars brought us alongside of the monster as he floated on the surface of the stream. The business was to attach a line to one of his legs; and as we knew that he was not dead, but only stunned, this was rather a nervous operation. I noticed indeed a hesitation among the men, as to who should venture, and fearing lest our prize should escape, I seized the line and made it fast to one of his fore-legs, when we proceeded to the shore, dragging him alongside. Before reaching it, however, our friend gave signs of reviving animation, and as we could not foresee to what extent he might regain his activity, we dropped him astern, clear of the boat, fearing lest in floundering about he might stave in her broadside. In doing so, moreover, and by way of a sedative, I fired a charge of large shot at his head, the muzzle of the gun not being a yard from it; and yet the only effect produced, was a slight stupor of the intellectual faculties, evinced by a momentary state of quiescence—On reaching the shore, the men jumped out to haul the alligator up on the dry land, and began to pull away vigorously. It was a comic scene to witness. They expected to have some difficulty in performing their task; but suddenly they found the rope slacken, and looking round beheld the alligator walking up after them of his own accord, faster than was pleasant. In their haste, endeavouring to keep the rope taut, one fellow tripped up; and it was for a moment a question whether or not he would be snapped in two; the feeling of alarm, however, soon gave way to a sense of the ludicrous, at beholding the manner in which he gathered himself up into a ball and rolled out of the alligator's way. I thought it now high time to take decisive measures, and with another shot altered the intentions of the monster, who endeavoured to back towards the water . . .

It was not before he had received six balls in the head that he consented to be killed. During the operation he exhibited something of his *savoir faire*, by opening his mouth, that looked like a giant man-trap, and suddenly shutting it with a loud snap, which made us shudder, and forcibly recalled to mind the escape I had had a few days before, from having my body embraced by such a pair of jaws . . .

All the alligator's stomach contained was about fourteen pounds of pebbles, some of them measuring four inches in diameter. We were some time skinning the monster, and after securing a little of the best part of the flesh for eating* proceeded on our way.

*The writer supped off alligator steaks, and informs the reader that the meat is by no means bad, and has a white appearance like veal.

Although the saltwater crocodile species had been recognised and classified—*Crocodylus porosus* was first described by the German naturalist Johann Gottlob Schneider in 1801—when the skull arrived at the British Museum in London, it was initially misidentified as an Indian Mugger (*Crocodylus palustris*). John Edward Gray, keeper of zoology at the museum from 1840 until 1874, wrote: 'The skull of this specimen, which was presented to the British Museum by Captain Stokes, has exactly the same form and proportions as that of the crocodiles called Goa and Muggar on the Indian continent, and is quite distinct in the characters from the Egyptian species . . . Messrs. Dumeril and Bib[e]ron deny that any species of crocodile is found in Australia.' (See Appendix 2 for John Edward Gray's full report)

A.M.C. Dumeril and G. Biberon were highly respected French zoologists who worked together classifying reptiles. They had concluded there were no crocodiles in Australia because it had been settled in the cooler south where there are, indeed, no crocodiles. However the *Beagle*, as Helpman so often rejoiced, was surveying uncharted territory, and it is possible that this very animal is the one that informed the world that Australia was home to huge populations of what would eventually be recognised as the largest reptile on earth, the saltwater crocodile.

On 23 November 1839, Helpman recorded the official naming of the great river where this crocodile was found, his use of capital letters portraying his excitement:

> THIS RIVER WAS DISCOVERED BY THE OFFICERS OF H.M.SLOOP 'BEAGLE' ON THE 18th OCTOBER 1839, AND WAS NAMED 'THE VICTORIA RIVER' IN HONOR OF HER MAJESTY THE QUEEN OF ENGLAND.

But by the end of the survey of this second major river system, Helpman was very much feeling the effects of the deprivations which were part and parcel of such explorations in the nineteenth century.

> None of my sores will heal; every scratch festers. 'Tis now 6 months since we left Sydney, 5 of which we have been on salt Provisions, so that I have no doubt we shall soon be Corned. How long I may keep, God knows. The constant perspirations weaken me dreadfully, and I am getting thinner than ever, black and spleenish.

By January 1840, Helpman and the *Beagle* were back in Fremantle, where they parted company.

Benjamin Francis Helpman now chose to make his home in the country he had first described as a 'barren, sterile and beastly place'. He left HMS *Beagle* and the Royal Navy to take a commission as the Commander of the West Australian Colonial Schooner, *Champion*, charged with surveying the West Australian coast and delivering stores to outlying settlements.

While surveying the northern rivers, Helpman made reference to colony gossip, 'Miss Pace has refused the Purser of the "Pelorus"!!! I am quite pleased by her taste'. His beloved Sarah now well and truly off the scene, it can only be assumed this is Miss Ann Pace, whom Helpman married in 1842 and who gave him nine children.

Having many times recorded his dismay that it would be three years before he saw his beloved homeland again, seventeen years would pass before Helpman returned to England. That was only for a brief visit to collect a new steamer, also named the *Champion*, which Helpman then commanded on trade routes along the Victorian coast. The *Champion* sank after a collision with the *Lady Bird* off Cape Otway, with the loss of thirty-two lives. Official enquiries were unable to conclude who was at fault, and no charges were laid.

In 1861 Helpman was appointed Harbour Master at Warrnambool, a role he performed until the post was abolished eight years later when he retired. He died in Warrnambool in 1874.

Throughout this long and productive life, I wonder if any day surpassed the one he claimed to be the happiest of his life—the day he first saw 'Alligators' on the Adelaide River.

2 AROUND THE WORLD, IN LIFE AND LEGEND

When Pikuwa was ill, he was alone except for Otama the porpoise. Pikuwa gasped for water. The porpoise told him to drink the salt water as he does. Pikuwa lamented that he wanted fresh water. Otama told him to dig a well for the crocodile has claws and digs in the mud, which the porpoise cannot do.

Pikuwa snapped at Otama who stabbed back with his spear. Pikuwa ran to his home, for he was but a coward. Pikuwa's son's wife came to help and rubbed his side where it was sore while she sang the crocodile song to him. Pikuwa accepted her ministrations as a declaration of love and took her for his wife.

The mother of the young woman came to tend and stroke Pikuwa's wound. He took her also to be his wife. Then came his sister's daughter, who Pikuwa also took to be his wife. Then he took as his wife his niece's mother and his own mother and his grandmother and all of his female relatives who came near.

Despite all the pleasures of his many women, he was distracted when Old Man Porpoise came and told him of a bandicoot which had gone into a hole. Pikuwa put his hand, which is his claw, into the hole and grabbed the bandicoot. But the bandicoot would not come. He tugged and he pulled but he could not pull the bandicoot from the hole and he would not let go. And so Pikuwa died.

Tales such as this reveal how closely the specific behaviour of the species of a region can inspire the legends which surround these amazing creatures. This is the case with the stories of crocodilians around the world. The legend of Pikuwa not only illustrates the indigenous storyteller's understanding that the crocodile species they were observing could live in both freshwater and saltwater habitats, but also reflects the male's tendency to collect a harem of females.

We have already met the 'saltie', one of the largest crocodilians. Although its common name reflects its preferences for coastal waters and the estuaries of large, tidal rivers, the saltie can be found well up the freshwater rivers of Northern Australia. However, the dominant species in the freshwater inland river systems is Australia's second native crocodilian, *Crocodylus johnstoni*, the Australian freshwater crocodile. At a maximum of 3 metres in length, the freshwater crocodile is dwarfed by its massive cousin. Predominantly a fish-eater, it digs hole nests and is generally shy of humans. When the saltwater crocodiles were heavily hunted and their populations declined, the smaller freshwater crocodiles expanded their range to reach some saline waterways but they have now retreated to their original freshwater habitats with the recovery of saltwater crocodile populations.

The success and wide distribution of the saltwater crocodile relates partly to its ability to thrive in almost any reasonably large aquatic environment, and partly to their unrivalled tolerance among their kind for travelling at sea. The saltie doesn't swim so much as drift in the open waters, and some have been recorded as travelling over a thousand kilometres. A few individuals have been found with barnacles on their scales, indicative of long sea voyages. In Australia, this crocodile is found in both saltwater and freshwater habitats, from the coast to inland rivers. It is found in billabongs and swamps, and by crossing land or travelling around the coast to new inlets or rivers, it spreads and colonises. The saltwater crocodile, also known as the estuarine crocodile, is found as far afield as Vanuatu and into parts of India.

The New Guinea crocodile (*Crocodylus novaeguineae*) is found across the large island which now consists of Papua New Guinea and the Indonesian province of Irian Jaya. It is a small to medium-sized crocodile and is found mostly in freshwater swamps, marshes and lakes. It is primarily nocturnal, feeding on fish, waterbirds, amphibians and smaller reptiles.

Although its range overlaps that of the much larger saltwater crocodile, unsurprisingly, they are rarely found together.

The Kikori people from the south of Papua New Guinea tell of the creation of the land by the New Guinea freshwater crocodile.

In the beginning the world was just water. In the water there lived a huge crocodile and he was God. When God gave birth to man and woman, there was no land on which they could live. The only place they could make their home was on his back. They bred in such great numbers that soon there was no room left on his back. The crocodile ordered them to leave his back. There was no land but there were great islands of crocodile dung. The people made their home on these islands. There they were able to grow all they required for the land was very fertile. They could fish the ocean and farm the land, and thus there was an abundance of food. These were the islands of Papua New Guinea where all of mankind started.

The legend tells of a crocodile which provides food, but offers no threat. This is the New Guinea freshwater crocodile.

Many of the renowned wood carvings of the various tribes that live along the Sepik River and its tributaries depict the ubiquitous crocodile, often revealing the unique cultural relationship that each village has with it. The Iatmul people of the magnificent Middle Sepik River, for example, revere the saltwater crocodile as the creator of the land and all living things.

In the beginning the world was covered with water. The first crocodile created dry land. This crocodile was a male. He caused a crack to appear in the newly formed dry earth. This was the female. The crocodile mated with the female and from their union came plants, animals and humans. When the lower jaw of the first crocodile fell to earth, the upper jaw rose to become the sky and the first dawn broke.

The Iatmul then tell of the ancestral crocodiles that roamed the land and founded their villages, witness to the fact that the crocodile is an animal that can travel widely if forced to by territorial battles and dry spells. In recognition of its ability to kill humans, the initiation ceremony of the young Iatmul men portrays the swallowing of the youths by the primeval crocodile, which then regurgitates them as men. The skin on some parts of their bodies is cut to represent the teeth marks of the crocodile.

From the Western Province of Papua New Guinea comes a story which tells how the various parts of the crocodile were named.

There was a small village, not far from the mouth of the Oriomo River, consisting of three families with eleven children. Their totem was the crocodile. Whenever the parents went to work in the gardens, the children would be minded by a very old man, the oldest person in the village. He was very conscientious, never letting the children stray from his sight. There was only one boy, Gaizu. One day, Gaizu's father uncovered a crocodile egg while out hunting. In the rare case of a single crocodile egg being laid, the egg is known to be very special.

Gaizu's father built a special pen for the egg on the muddy riverside, and watched over it carefully. The egg finally hatched, and the tiny crocodile was given to Gaizu as a pet. All the children loved the little crocodile. They named her Aka, the word for grandmother, because they loved her as they did their own grandmothers.

Aka grew and grew, and before long the children realised she could take them for a ride on her back. They waited eagerly for their parents to go to the gardens and leave them with only the old man to watch them, and then, for the first time, they let Aka out of her pen. They begged Aka to take them for a ride on the river, and she did.

Gaizu took up his position at the front of Aka's head, right on top of the nostrils. Sabui, Kuikit, Kayut-dan and Nataru-kubi sat in that order on her head. Nubeza and Za-nubesa sat on her back while Adata, Ulaita and Mopata sat on her tail. The parts of the crocodile are known by the children's names today.

Aka took them down to the mouth of the river and, when the tide turned, she brought them back to the village. No-one knew of their adventures except the old man who could not stop them. Many times, when their parents were away, the children rode the crocodile to the mouth of the river and home again. When their parents finally learned of the children's journeys, they were unable to stop them.

One day, Aka swam beyond the mouth of the river and out to sea where she fed on seaweed and grass. When they returned home, Gaizu was very cross with her. He demanded she open her mouth, took the remains of the seaweed and grass from her throat, and threw them in her face. The old man rebuked him, for he knew that the crocodile would become bad tempered.

Each time they returned, Gaizu would take the seaweed and grass from Aka's mouth and throw it at her. The old man became more worried. Eventually, Aka became so angry she took the children far out to sea, where she lowered her body down in the water. The children begged her to stop, for they were getting wet, but she took no notice. Aka called all the crocodiles and sharks in the sea to join her, then she started to swim. She swam and swam, further and further from their village. The children begged her to take them home but she still took no notice.

The old man watched from the top of a mangrove tree, knowing they would never return. When Aka had swum past the island of Bobo, Gaizu called to her to stop at the reef he could see ahead. But the foam was not a reef. It was the sharks and crocodiles Aka had called. With a splash so huge the old man could see it from his far-off mangrove tree, Aka tossed the children into the water, into the mouths of her waiting friends. They were all eaten.

The old man told the parents all that had happened. They faced the island of Bobo and wept for their lost children. Aka was never seen again.

The crocodile of this tale, which swims from the rivers into the sea and eats people, is the saltwater crocodile. There are Papuan tribes which believe that people eaten by crocodiles can be seen in the eyes of the predator at night. Like many nocturnal animals, crocodilian eyes reflect light shone on them at night producing an eerie pair of lights on the water's surface. Should the possessed crocodile trouble the villagers, they will lure the animal up river and then return home across country, taking advantage of the crocodile's need to be always near water.

The Indonesian province of Irian Jaya occupies the western half of the island which is also home to Papua New Guinea. From there comes the story of the magic crocodile—a story of a flood which has a very familiar rhythm to it.

Once, it is told, Towjatuwa came from his village of Sawja to the Tami River in search of a smooth stone. In those days, it was believed a mother giving birth would almost surely die. To aid the birth an operation using a stone adze was used which would almost certainly lead to her death. Towjatuwa came to find such a stone for his child was soon to be born. He was very sad, for he loved his wife.

As he searched, he heard a voice behind him. He turned to find a huge crocodile walking towards him. On his back were not only the scales of a crocodile but also the feathers of a cassowary. Towjatuwa was very frightened but he was calmed by the friendly voice of the crocodile, so he explained why he was searching for a stone. The crocodile assured him that the operation was not necessary and offered to accompany Towjatuwa home and help with the birth. In this way, the crocodile said, his wife would not die.

Overjoyed, Towjatuwa and his wife made the crocodile welcome. The crocodile covered the woman's body with the special herbs and medicines he had carried in his mouth. The boy child was born naturally and safely and all was well. Towjatuwa asked the crocodile, whose name was Watuwe, to name the boy, and he did so, calling the child Narrowra.

Watuwe then told them of the future when Narrowra would be grown into a fine hunter. He told of his own death at the hands of the hunters who would eat his flesh. This would cause anger in the heart of the god, Kwembo, who would cause great waters to flood the earth. He told Towjatuwa and Narrowra that they must not eat him, but ask for his scrotum which they must take high onto the mountain where the Angels of the Sky would tell them what they must do.

All happened as the crocodile had predicted. The villagers killed the crocodile after they became aware of his presence when he parted the waters of the Tami River to extinguish a fire lit there by children. They killed the huge crocodile with the cassowary feathers between its scales as it tried to extinguish the flames. The crocodile was so huge that all the villagers feasted upon its meat and called those from nearby villages to join in their luck.

Towjatuwa had been away when the crocodile was killed, and on returning passed his share of the meat to another, asking only for the scrotum. With Narrowra, Narrowra's sister, a friend and his sister, Towjatuwa climbed Mount Sankria. There he beheld the beauty of the Jankwenk, the Angels of the Sky. The Angels told him that all the people of the earth would be destroyed for killing Watuwe. Towjatuwa and his small group would rebuild the earth with the animals, plants and seeds now given to them. The Angels turned to the four points of the compass and blew upon their flutes. Instead of music, a deafening noise summoned the waters to flood the earth. Storms raged, and all that was saved were those few on the top of Mount Sankria.

Under the only remaining tree, an ironwood on Mount Sankria, Towjatuwa released a kangaroo which returned, so Towjatuwa knew the waters had not yet subsided. A few days later, he released a parrot, which also returned. When a pig was released a few days later, it did not return.

Narrowra spread the banana seeds the Angels had given him. From the banana trees, which grew instantly, the small group of people cut the stems. Narrowra commanded the stems to become women of many shapes and sizes. They began to build homes. Narrowra scattered more banana seeds and from the stems then cut, he commanded men of many shapes and sizes to arise. The men were sent to hunt for pigs.

Towjatuwa found the women dancing. He told the men to dance with the women. The men then climbed into the homes, where Narrowra told the men to blow their flutes. This frightened the women who wanted to run away, but Narrowra had taken their ladders so they could not escape.

The men then decorated themselves with squares on their bodies like the scales of a crocodile. They put feathers on their heads from the cassowary, and a frame of rattan reaching a metre above their heads and the feathers of the white cockatoo. And atop it all was a live cassowary. They danced to the shrill sounds of the flute, and the women became curious. Narrowra paired the small men with the small women and the large men with the large women. He gave them seeds including sago, and told them to scatter and bring into being the villages of the area.

When the women discovered the sacred part of Watuwe which had been hidden in a special container, things started to go wrong. Narrowra scolded them, decreeing that the people of the new villiage, Arso, should care for the part of Watuwe, tying it to a branch of the great ironwood tree from the very top of Mount Sankria. In this way they took it home to Arso, where it was placed in a room where only men may go.

It has been guarded ever since for if it is ever damaged, the people surely believe, another great flood will come. And this is the tale of the magic crocodile, Watuwe.

Travelling on from Papua New Guinea and Irian Jaya we come to Timor. The young country of East Timor won its hard-fought independence in 2002 and occupies the eastern end of the island of Timor. This small island is rich in culture and legend and many Timorese live according to an animist belief system known as *Lulik*, in which spirits and ancestors live alongside mortals in a sacred world. The crocodile is revered by the Timorese, as can be seen in this story of the creation of the island of Timor.

A young crocodile lived in a swamp, far from the sea. There was little to eat in the small swamp so the crocodile knew he would stay small. One day he decided to travel across the land in search of the sea so he could grow large on the food there. As the day became hot, he was still far from the shore. He started to dry out and knew he would soon die. A small boy found the failing creature and gently took him to the sea and safety. The crocodile vowed to be loyal to the boy. When the crocodile had grown large and strong, the small boy had become a man. He wanted to travel the world and sought the help of the one he called 'Brother Crocodile'. The crocodile told the young man to climb on his back and they set off east in the oceans. They travelled for years. Eventually the crocodile told the man the time had come for him to die. In return for the man's kindness, he declared he would turn himself into a beautiful island where the man and his children could live until the sun sinks into the sea. As he died, the crocodile grew and grew, until he became an island. His ridged back became the mountains and his scales became the hills of Timor.

No-one can dispute that the geography of Timor resembles the shape of a crocodile. However this legend is also an accurate observation of the behaviour of the saltwater or estuarine crocodile of the region. Those who live in a restricted waterhole remain small. When a swamp or waterhole dries up, they will cross land seeking better water, running the risk of dehydration and death from heat exposure. As we have seen, this particular species of crocodile is the only one which can sustain long trips in the ocean.

We now move into the Asian region, north-west of Australia, where the ubiquitous saltwater crocodile is joined by other crocodilians. The Siamese crocodile (*Crocodylus siamensis*) was once widespread in the countries surrounded by the Indian Ocean, the South China Sea and the Philippine Sea, but is now under real threat of extinction in the wild, with Cambodia the last stronghold for the threatened population. The Siamese crocodile can reach up to 4 metres in length, but rarely does so. With numbers dwindling in the wild, very little is known of its natural biology. Habitat destruction and the collection of wild females for farming are the principal causes of its demise. Active conservation work is underway, but there are no immediate solutions on the horizon.

Indonesia and Malaysia are also home to the tomistoma (*Tomistoma schlegelii*), or false gharial. It has the characteristic slender snout of the gharial, found further to the west on the subcontinent but, despite continuing dispute, it is currently classified as a 'true' crocodile. Growing to 5 metres or more, this is a large crocodilian which reportedly feeds on everything from fish to macaque monkeys, although its elongated, narrow snout is more typical of specialist fish-eaters.

In the south Moluccas, a group of islands in the Molucca Sea, there are puberty rites which embrace the crocodile character. Young males pass through the jaws of a replica crocodile, leaving their mothers to grieve their loss. They spend time with the priests being initiated into the tribal secrets, before their return to the village to much rejoicing, their lives having been spared by the crocodile. It is not hard to imagine that in the region of the saltwater crocodile, youths were often taken when first they went to sea or into the rivers to catch food. While the mothers are proud to release their sons to their adult roles within the tribe, the symbolic use of the crocodile acknowledges the loss of their child.

Many countries have stories of young virgins being sacrificed to crocodiles. Others tell of the way crocodiles will take the young virgins from a group of women washing at the water's edge. What is more likely is that the crocodile targets the smallest person, or the one on the outskirts of the group. Humans are a large prey for crocodiles, whose preference for smaller mammals is well known. A small animal at the edge of a group is more vulnerable and it is probably this, rather than a girl's virginity, which attracts a crocodile.

An Indonesian legend takes place at the water's edge and, though it involves a crocodile, it otherwise shows striking similarities to the western tale of Cinderella.

Damura lived with her father, her stepmother and her stepsister. One day Damura's stepmother sent her to the river to wash clothes. While washing the clothes Damura lost a garment in the water. A crocodile emerged from the water and Damura greeted it politely. Pleased by this, the crocodile not only vowed not to eat her, but offered to help Damura if she would look after her young. Damura sang to the baby crocodile until the mother returned with the lost garment.

The crocodile told Damura to open her mouth. She dropped something into it, and told the young girl to speak to no-one on the road home. When she reached her home, Damura greeted her father and two gold coins dropped from her mouth. Immediately Damura's stepsister went to the river. She pretended to lose a garment, and the mother crocodile appeared. She asked the girl to mind the baby while she searched for the lost garment. The stepsister sang a nasty song to the baby crocodile, accusing it of smelling awful. On her return home, only stones fell from her mouth.

One day the king asked everyone to feast with him, but Damura's stepmother told her to stay at home. Damura went once more to the crocodile for help. The crocodile clothed Damura in a sarong, a jacket of golden silk and golden sandals. Damura then disobeyed her stepmother and went to the feast, and the prince fell in love with her. When the cock crowed to announce the dawn, Damura fled, but the prince caught hold of one golden sandal. He searched for the girl to whom the sandal belonged, and found Damura and proposed marriage.

The angry stepmother threw Damura into the river, but the crocodile returned her to the arms of her prince.

The Philippine crocodile (*Crocodylus mindorensis*) is a relatively small species, living mostly in small lakes, ponds, river tributaries and marshes on a limited number of islands in the Philippines. It was once found all over the Philippines, but commercial exploitation and habitat destruction have caused it to become a severely endangered species. A decade ago it was feared there were no more than a hundred mature crocodiles in the wild. The Philippine crocodiles build a mound to nest, and both the eggs and the crocodiles are collected by local farmers. Given the poverty of the region it is hard to ask them to do otherwise, but they are now encouraged to sell the crocodiles to crocodile farms which, along with zoos and other captive breeding programs, may be the only chance this species has of survival.

The Philippine crocodile's territory overlaps that of the much larger and more dangerous saltwater crocodile, and so local legends may reflect either species. Every area has its own cultural relationship with crocodiles. Some traditional communities in the Philippines, such as the Panay, revere the crocodile so highly that it is taboo to kill it. Other tribes see the crocodile as the reincarnation of a respected person who has died. Asingan, a town in the Philippine province of Pangasinan, has a legend about a huge crocodile and the river.

Every Saturday morning the women went to the river to wash clothes. One Saturday, late in the afternoon, a young woman found a crocodile behind her. His approach had been silent. With only a brief scream and a splash, the young woman disappeared. Horrified, those with her at the river's edge saw only the scaled back and tail of the crocodile as it sank swiftly into the water with its prey. The frightened women took the dreadful news back to the village. The girl's father led a search party, discovering his daughter in a nearby clearing, weak but still alive. Hysterical, and with her leg badly mauled, she said the crocodile had brought her to its hiding place. There, in a small cave in the river bank, far away from the village, she had been dumped among the skeletons of many humans and animals. She realised the animal had just eaten and so was keeping her for its next meal. Playing dead, the young girl waited for the crocodile to leave. She crept out of the cave and escaped. Exhausted, she lost consciousness until her father found her.

The young girl guided the men of the village to the crocodile's lair, where they captured the huge beast with strong ropes. Consumed with fear and hatred for the creature, they beat it until it died. The river saw everything and she was not pleased for the crocodile was one of her children. Dragging the crocodile to the village square, the men stripped its skin and fed the dogs with its meat. The remains of the creature were buried in the middle of the square.

That night, the river wailed mournfully, like a mother mourning a lost child. The river was pleading to the heavens asking for help. At midnight, a typhoon caused the river to break its banks. Next morning, the townspeople found the houses near the river were swept away. The river had become a flood of trees and houses, for it could not forgive what had been done to the crocodile. Every year, at the time of the killing of her child, a strong typhoon comes and the river floods the land. Every year the river comes closer and closer to the village square, trying to reclaim the bones of the crocodile. It will not stop until it succeeds.

The legend of Asingan is a fascinating reflection of the behaviour of the crocodile, and it almost certainly refers to the saltwater crocodile because of the deadly nature of the attack. Suddenly and silently taking the smallest animal in a group at the water's edge is typical crocodilian behaviour, and it is not surprising that the survivor of such an attack would go down in legend. As we shall see in later chapters, crocodiles are opportunist hunters and gorge feeders and will gorge until completely full and then store the rest in the water until they can consume more. Also, prolonged immersion in the water softens the carcass's connective tissue, which some claim makes it easier for the crocodile to break it up. The enraged killing of the crocodile would have been a traumatic event in the life and history of the village, so it is easy to see how the death of the crocodile could be linked to the seasonal hurricanes and flooding of the river to create a powerful legend.

As we leave the Philippines and travel on to China, we meet the first crocodilian who is not considered a 'true' crocodile. The Chinese alligator (*Alligator sinensis*) population is isolated from other crocodilians, and only a few hundred individuals are estimated to live in a handful of scattered populations around the Yangtze River. Like its nearest relative, the American alligator, the Chinese alligator lives in more temperate climates than the other crocodilians. It survives the cold winter months by hibernating in burrows, which form part of the complex tunnel systems it digs along the river banks. The temperature within these burrows rarely falls below 10°C and, in fact, the Chinese alligator spends over half of the year underground. Tunnels from the burrows lead down to entrances which are below the water level. Unfortunately this means that when the Yangtze floods, as it did in 1987, many of the alligators drown.

The Chinese who share their river banks with the alligator have no fear for their personal safety as it is a small, timid animal which has never been known to attack humans. At less than 2 metres long, the alligator's staple diet is fish, turtles and frogs. Unfortunately tolerance towards alligators is not high when they attack the farmers' ducks and chickens, and dig burrows into their fields.

Widely believed to be the source of the mystical tradition of dragons in China's art and literature, the first mention of the Chinese alligator is found in the writings of Marco Polo, published in 1299. Almost certainly observed coming out of hibernation in spring and disappearing into its burrows for the winter, the dragon is described in Chinese literature as the lord of all scaled reptiles, ascending into the heavens at the spring equinox and plunging into the waters at the autumn equinox. It is told that about four thousand years ago, the sage Fu His encountered a dragon as it emerged from the Yangtze River. It tutored him in the art of writing. On its back there appeared to be letters which he noted down. These became mystic symbols used for centuries after.

A supernatural beast, the dragon has appeared in many forms: robust, elegantly thin, large and more petite. The Chinese sign for the dragon first appears during the Shang (or Yin) dynasty, which spanned the sixteenth to the eleventh centuries BC. In the earliest Chinese records, in inscriptions on bones and turtle shields, the dragon is depicted as a horned reptile with teeth, scales and, at times, paws. Above the sign there may be a further symbol indicating violence and evil.

As time passed, the depictions of dragons became more ornate and imaginative. The dragon was described as having a spiny back and scales down its side, prominent claws and a flat head. But this alligator-like creature also had antlers like those of a deer. Claws more like eagle's talons and the sinuous neck of a snake join ears like those of a buffalo and the head of a camel to create a creature which has become a montage of the animal kingdom rather than the representation of a single beast. Ancient texts refer to this assembly of parts. For example, quoting Wang Fu of the Eastern Han Dynasty in his 'Literary Expositor', Luo Yuan of the Southern Song Dynasty (1127–1279 AD) wrote:

> . . . depictions of creatures with the head of a horse and body of a snake are commonly considered dragon images. But dragons actually have three sections and nine likenesses. The three connected sections are from the head to the upper leg, the leg to the abdomen, and the abdomen to the tail. The nine likenesses are horns of a stag, head of a camel, eyes of a demon, neck of a snake, belly of a clam, scales of a fish, talons of an eagle, paws of a tiger, and ears of an ox.

Worshipped and revered over the centuries, the dragon has become an ever more wondrous beast, one which still inspires Chinese creativity and ethnic traditions.

Scholars who have analysed the earliest depictions of the dragon consider it to be highly reptilian, with its alligator-like characteristics dominant. Without immediate assistance, however, the creature which has inspired so much wonderful art, mythology and literature may disappear, leaving only memories of its true existence. Fortuately it does breed well in captivity and a small breeding colony has been established in Louisiana, USA, but to lose the wild animal which inspired such a rich tradition would be a tragedy.

Although the indigenous range of the Chinese alligator is now very limited, legend indicates it may once have been much broader. On the mainland of Japan, across the Sea of Japan from Korea, is the Grand Shrine of Okuninushi at Izumo-taisha. The most famous story in the series of legends about Okuninushi, the Izumo Cycle, is that of the White Rabbit.

Okuninushi was attending his eighty brothers who all sought the love of the beautiful princess, Ya-gami-hime of Inaba. Finding a rabbit without fur, clearly in great pain, the brothers advised the rabbit to bathe in salt water, which only served to make it worse. Okuninushi asked the rabbit his story. The rabbit had wanted to cross from the island of Oki, in the Sea of Japan, to Izumo. There was no bridge, so the rabbit had persuaded a family of crocodiles to form a living bridge to enable him to cross the water. He had promised that he would count the number of crocodiles, who were to lie end to end, and compare them to the number of sea creatures, so the crocodiles could know which were more numerous. But this was just a ruse to fool the crocodiles into forming the bridge. Just before he had completed the crossing, the foolish rabbit told this to the crocodiles. In a rage, the last crocodile in the bridge skinned the rabbit alive. Okuninushi told the rabbit that he should instead bathe in the fresh water of the river mouth and roll on ground sprinkled with the pollen of the Kama grass. The rabbit was in fact a deity. When the cure worked and the rabbit's snow white fur returned, he rewarded Okuninushi with the hand of Ya-gami-hime.

How much can we interpret from this legend? Does the story originate from the extended range of the Chinese alligator into that region? In which case, does this mean that the alligator was found in the salt water of the Japan Sea? Or does this story arise from the travels of people who take their stories with them?

Maybe there is another explanation. In 1690, the German explorer Engelbert Kaempfer, told of an encounter in Japan with what he described as a living dragon. It seems likely that he did see a captive crocodilian in a shrine. Given the climate, it is almost certain that it would have been the Chinese alligator and not a tropical crocodile species. Perhaps young alligators, brought to Japan as curios or gifts for the Emperor's menagerie, were the basis of such stories.

As we travel through Indochina to the great subcontinent, we enter the territory of the marsh crocodile (*Crocodylus palustris*) or, to give it its wonderfully evocative common name, the mugger. The name probably derives from the Hindi word *magar*, meaning 'water monster'. Despite its broad snout, the mugger is not an alligator but a 'true' crocodile. It can reach up to 5 metres in length and is found across India, Sri Lanka and Bangladesh, as well as in parts of Pakistan, Iran and Nepal. The mugger's natural habitats are freshwater lakes, marshes and rivers, but it is an adaptive animal and can also be found in irrigation canals and man-made reservoirs. The mugger also adapts its diet to its surroundings. Its usual prey is fish, amphibians and reptiles, but it will eat monkeys and even larger mammals such as deer and buffalo.

The mugger has been worshipped for centuries. Believed to be the servant of Krishnu, the crocodile has great spiritual significance and there are many shrines where the Sufi Islamic devotees come to seek healing and pray. In the famous shrine, Manghopir, near the Pakistani port city of Karachi, the mugger pit is a popular tourist attraction. The Manghopir shrine is believed to be the resting place of Baba Farid Shakar Ganj, a thirteenth-century Sufi saint. Manghopir was a Hindu bandit who tried to rob the saint's caravan. Realising his sin, he converted from Hinduism to Islam and was rewarded by Ganj who rid him of his lice. When Manghopir bathed in what was then a hot spring, he shook his head and his lice fell into the water and turned into crocodiles.

The crocodiles are reputed to have lived in the muddy pond at Manghopir for seven centuries and now number about 150. Pilgrims to what is, essentially, a crocodile sanctuary feed the animals with beef, mutton or chicken in the hope they will be rewarded with the fulfilment of their wishes.

India is also home to the gharial (*Gavialis gangeticus*), a very different animal to the mugger. One of the largest of the crocodilian species, often approaching 6 metres in length, it is clumsy on land but very agile in water. The biggest difference between the gharial and the mugger is in their snouts, the gharial having a slender, elongated snout and needle-like teeth, perfect for catching the fish that form the mainstay of its diet. The bulbous growth on the tip of its snout that gives it its name is called a *ghara* after the Indian word for 'pot'.

The gharial is found primarily across the northern Indian subcontinent; an isolated population has been found in Pakistan, too, although its survival is now in some doubt. In 1974, the estimated total adult gharial population in the world was only about 150, so the gharial has come perilously close to extinction. A conservation program instigated in India in 1975, and in Nepal in 1978, involves collecting eggs in the wild and incubating them in research stations. This program has successfully hatched thousands of young, who are reared in captivity for the first few years of life before being released into the wild. Rising gharial populations indicate that these young gharials are successfully repopulating their traditional territories.

The gharial has been tainted with the epithet 'man-eater', perhaps because human remains and jewellery have been found in the stomachs of some specimens. However, many zoologists believe that the gharials, opportunist feeders like all crocodilians, may be taking advantage of the Hindu custom of consigning their dead to the Ganges River.

Many Indian folk legends feature the gharial, particularly in partnership with its adversary the monkey. One tells of a friendship which grew between a gharial and a monkey on the banks of the Ganges.

The monkey would bring the fruit of his home to the gharial. Smelling of roses and tasting like apple, it was called a rose-apple. The two creatures became firm friends as they shared the monkey's fruit each day.

The gharial took the fruit home to his wife. On tasting the sweet fruit and hearing of its origin, she decided the heart of the monkey must be sweet from eating so many rose-apples. She asked her husband to bring home the monkey so that she might eat its heart. He cried out that the monkey was his friend, but to no avail. He blew bubbles and made sounds from his bulbous nose, but still she wanted the heart of the monkey. He finally agreed and invited the monkey home for dinner, offering his back for the ride. The monkey protested that he could not swim. He would drown, he said, as they travelled to the gharial's home. But the gharial assured his friend that he would be safe as he lived on a sunny island in the river. So the monkey came bearing rose-apples to give to the gharial's wife. Before the gharial reached his home, his guilt overcame him and he confessed the plan. The monkey exclaimed that he had left his heart in the tree, and he would retrieve it if the gharial took him back. The monkey sped up his tree, refusing to visit the gharial again. The gharial told his wife that the little monkey had drowned on the trip, and he never got to taste rose-apples again.

Again, this legend reflects observed behaviour. Gharials often take their catch, whether fish or an unwary monkey, back to nests or lairs where it is stored, sometimes for days. They are agile in the water, but perhaps the most ungainly of the crocodilians on land, especially when compared to a monkey. The gharial uses the bulbous growth on his snout to make a resonant hum, and to blow bubbles during the mating ritual.

Further westward, to the next crocodilian home in our travels—Egypt. The Nile crocodile (*Crocodylus niloticus*) is a giant among crocodilians. It is quite common for adult males to reach 6 metres in length, and there are unsubstantiated reports of even larger individuals. That being said, this particular species displays a great deal of variation over its range, which is well beyond the reaches of the Nile River. In fact, the Nile crocodile can be found in most of Africa, excepting the north-west of the country, and even in Madagascar.

The Nile crocodile is perhaps the most dangerous of the crocodilians to humans, as it makes no distinction between man and beast as prey. Although it will, in common with other crocodilians, take a dwarf form if confined to small waterways or in captivity, in the mighty river which dominates Egypt, the Nile, crocodiles reign supreme.

One of the earliest descriptions of the crocodile comes from the Greek historian and chronicler Herodotus, who travelled extensively in Egypt in the fifth century BC.

> I will now show what kind of creature is the crocodile. For the four winter months it eats nothing. It has four feet, and lives both on land and in the water, for it lays eggs and hatches them out on land, and it passes the greater part of the day on dry ground, and the night in the river, the water being warmer than the air and dew. No mortal creature known to us grows from so small a beginning to such greatness; for its eggs are not much bigger than goose eggs, and the young crocodile is a bigness answering thereto, but it grows to a length of seventeen cubits and more. It has eyes

like pigs' eyes, and great teeth and tusks answering to the bigness of its body. It is the only animal that has no tongue. Nor does it move the lower jaw. It is the only creature that brings the upper jaw down upon the lower. It also has strong claws, and a scaly impenetrable hide on its back. It is blind in the water, but very keen of sight in the air. Since it lives in the water, its mouth is all full within of leeches. All birds and beasts flee from it, except only the sandpiper, with which it is at peace, because this bird does the crocodile a service, for whenever the crocodile comes ashore out of the water and then opens its mouth (and this it does for the most part to catch the west wind), the sandpiper goes into its mouth and eats the leeches; the crocodile is pleased by this service and does the sandpiper no harm.

Some of the Egyptians hold crocodiles sacred, others do not so, but treat them as enemies. The dwellers about Thebes and the lake Moeris deem them to be very sacred. There, in every place one crocodile is kept, trained to be tame; they put ornaments of glass and gold on its ears and bracelets on its forefeet, provide for it special food and offerings, and give the creatures the best of treatment while they live; after death the crocodiles are embalmed and buried in sacred coffins. But about Elephantine they are not held scared, and are even eaten. The Egyptians do not call them crocodiles, but champsae. The Ionians call them crocodiles from their likeness to the lizards which they have on their walls.

Herodotus gives a fair account of the Nile crocodile, although it does not hibernate in winter, as Herodotus seems to suggest. It is less visible because its physical systems slow in the colder weather. This allows the crocodile to conserve its energy so it needs to feed less. Herodotus can be forgiven for thinking that the Nile crocodile has no tongue. In fact, like all crocodilians, the tongue is attached along the length of the lower jaw, so unless one is much closer to the crocodile than would be deemed prudent, it is very hard to see. The crocodile does move its lower jaw, but it tends to raise its head when biting. Seventeen cubits is about 8 metres, so perhaps the size of the animal has grown in the telling!

As the source of life, and death, to those who lived on the flood-rich soil of its banks, the Nile and its largest inhabitants were venerated by the ancient Egyptians. Crocodiles are significant in the pantheon of Egyptian gods. Most often depicted in wall paintings as a human figure with the head of a crocodile, Sobek or Sebek is the crocodile god—the god of power, protection and fertility. Crocodiles were considered to be Sobek's earthly representatives. The mummified remains of adults, hatchlings and even eggs have been found, evidence of the respect in which the animals were held. The ancient Greeks knew the Egyptian city of Medinet el Faiyum as Crocodilopolis, a centre of crocodile worship, possibly where Herodotus got some of his information.

While Sobek is, in many ways, a benign god, the crocodile head also belongs to the Devourer of Souls, a terrifying figure to the Egyptians. Ammut or Ammit is a female demon with the head of a crocodile, the torso of a leopard and the hindquarters of a hippopotamus. The Egyptian people believed that after death their souls were judged by Osiris, god of the dead, and weighed on the scales of Ma'at, goddess of law, order and truth. Those souls found to be more wicked than good were fed to Ammut, as she crouched beside the scales of justice. The ancient Egyptians were terrified at the prospect of their souls being judged unworthy, as this meant that they would have no prospect of reincarnation or a blissful afterlife with Osiris in the Fields of Peace.

Through their worship of Sobek and Ammut, the ancient Egyptians respected not only the crocodile's place in the fertile ecosystem of the Nile, but also the danger it posed, as an opportunist lurking in the shallows, always on the alert for prey. However, not all Nile crocodiles are so terrifying. As we have seen on our travels, large crocodilians will adapt their size to their surroundings. In Paga, a very small town on the border of Ghana and Burkina Faso, a town no-one would have heard of were it not for its crocodile ponds, the local people live safely with small Nile crocodiles. As often happens in cultures with a strong tradition of oral history, there are many stories of how this came about.

A hunter was being chased by a lion. The hunter came to the edge of a pond, where he begged a crocodile to protect him and help him to escape across the pond. In exchange, the hunter vowed he and his descendants would never eat the meat of a crocodile again. Having been helped by the crocodile to safety, the hunter decided to make his home on the edge of the pond and he established the village of Paga.

It is also told that the founder of Paga was a man by the name of Nave, who ran from his home because his dog had been killed for a sacrifice by his parents. Lost and thirsty, he was guided to the waterhole by a crocodile. There he settled and the village which grew around him is now called Paga. In respect for his guiding crocodile, Nave decreed that the crocodiles of the pond in Paga would never be eaten.

While there are many versions of the story, the consistent theme is that Paga's origins are closely associated with the crocodiles which are still central to the lives of the local people. There are many crocodiles in the pond, its surrounds and the nearby dams. These crocodiles are so accustomed to people that the villagers can wash and swim in the pond and feed the crocodiles. Children ride them and people, including visitors, handle them with impunity. It is believed that each descendent of the original hunter has a personal crocodile who will come to his doorstep on his death and die with him.

The Nile crocodile is also found in southern Africa. The Thonga tribe in Zululand use crocodile fat in their medicines to guard against both lightning and illness. They also wear a crocodile tooth or claw around their necks as an amulet to protect them from crocodile attacks and consider that the best protection is offered by a tooth or a claw from a man-eater.

When something is unusual it attracts attention, and around such rare events legends are woven. Albino crocodiles are known, but are certainly not common. One such white crocodile is possibly the source of an ongoing tradition from South Africa. The following legend is a beautiful example of the indigenous peoples' knowledge of the behaviour of the animals they revered. This legend refers to the gastroliths, the rocks found inside the stomachs of all adult crocodilians.

There once lived a white crocodile in Lake Fundunzi, near Limpopo, who was greatly revered by the VhaVenda people. The crocodile gained its strength from the stones it swallowed and carried in its stomach. Long ago, one of the chiefs of the VhaVenda tribe also swallowed a stone—a white stone. When the VhaVenda chief died, his body was placed high up on a burial stack on a sacred site. The body remained there until it completely decomposed and the white rock dropped to the ground. The sacred site was attended by the women of the tribe, who were not allowed to become chief and therefore would not be tempted to swallow the sacred rock. The rightful heir to the chief then swallowed the sacred rock, which granted him the strength and potency of the white crocodile of the lake.

The nineteenth-century explorer David Livingston reported the beliefs of the Crocodile Clan of South Africa. Known as the *Ba-kuena*, the clan venerated the crocodile as their traditional ancestor. They tried to avoid contact with crocodiles, believing them to cause swelling of the eyes (perhaps because of the bulbous nature of the crocodile's eyes) and blindness. Any member of the clan who survived a crocodile attack was believed to be more crocodile than human and rejected by the tribe. The clan also marked the ears of their cattle with the image of their ancestral crocodile.

Despite its prominence, the Nile crocodile is not the only crocodilian on the African continent. From northern Angola to Senegal, along the western coast of Africa, the slender-snouted crocodile (*Crocodylus cataphractus*) is found in densely forested rivers and large lakes. Its slender snout is ideal for its preferred prey—the fish and small aquatic invertebrates of its home waters. It usually does not exceed 2.5 metres in length, although the occasional larger specimen has been reported.

The western coast of Africa, from Guinea-Bissau down to Angola and inland to the Central African Republic and the Congo, is home to the African dwarf crocodile (*Osteolaemus tetraspis*). A solitary, nocturnal species, it measures less than 2 metres in length. Spending most of the day in burrows which, like those of the Chinese alligator, may be partially submerged, it is seldom seen. As a smaller, secretive animal in the country which boasts the dramatic Nile crocodile, it is not surprising that the dwarf crocodile is less likely to be reflected in African mythology.

In the west of Africa is the small country of Benin, where all three African species can be found. The indigenous stories tell of malignant spirits disguised as crocodiles which prey on travellers. It is probable that the malignant spirits were disguised as the Nile crocodile, and not its smaller and more timid relations. Crocodiles were kept in ponds near the royal palace and fed by a priest, perhaps reflecting the practices of Egypt.

As we continue west we come to South America, home of the caimans. Despite 'caiman' being the Spanish term for 'crocodile', caimans are not crocodiles. They are members of the alligator family, similar in appearance to the broad-snouted alligators. The most common of the caimans is called, unoriginally, the common caiman (*Caiman crocodilus*). It is also known as the spectacled caiman because of the bony ridges and light circles around its eyes. The common caiman has a wide range, from Brazil and Peru in the south, through Central America and into Mexico. A highly adaptable species, it is relatively small, with the largest recorded specimens rarely reaching 3 metres. The common caiman can change colour to a limited degree with the external temperature. Its proliferation, adaptability and range have led to a number of subspecies being defined, the exact number of which, as we shall see in Chapter 4, is still under dispute. It is reportedly never eaten by the native peoples of its area, who value crocodilian teeth and scales as powerful mystical symbols. The caiman is often referred to as an alligator, as in this story from Guyana where the Pomeroon Basin tribe tell how their tribe was created.

The Sun god was distressed because his fish kept disappearing from his ponds at night. He asked the alligator to guard his fish, not realising that the alligator was the very one who was stealing them. The Sun god finally caught the alligator in the act. He was enraged and slashed the alligator's skin, which led to scales being formed all over it. The alligator begged for his life, offering the Sun god his daughter for a wife. But the alligator was a liar; he had no daughter. When his offer was accepted, he was forced to carve a woman from a tree. She was not a complete woman and could not bear the Sun god sons. The alligator called on the woodpecker, who made the woman complete. A snake then emerged from between the woman's thighs. The Sun god accepted her as a true wife, and she bore him twin sons, founders of the tribe.

The northern countries of South America are also home to the smallest of the crocodilian species, with adult males rarely exceeding 1.5 metres in length. Healthy numbers of the heavily-armoured Cuvier's dwarf caiman (*Paleosuchus palpebrosus*) are found in a wide range of rivers across the continent. Schneider's dwarf caiman (*Paleosuchus trigonatus*) is slightly larger and, although its range overlaps that of the Cuvier's dwarf caiman in places, it is not as prolific.

The largest of the caimans is the black caimans (*Melanosuchus niger*) which is found in northern Brazil, parts of Bolivia, Peru, Ecuador, Colombia, French Guiana and

Guyana. This is a fairly large animal, with authenticated recordings of 4-metre males. There are unconfirmed reports of 6-metre individuals. The black caiman hunts by night, commonly venturing onto land to take mammals, and attacks on domestic animals and humans have been reported. The black caiman's numbers have been devastated by uncontrolled hunting.

Central Brazil is home to four species of caiman, but the black caiman would have been the inspiration for this wonderful tale from the Sherente tribe.

It is told of the seven brothers who were sent from their village as punishment for the trouble they had created. In the rainforest, they could find little food and no water. The creatures of the forest were fierce and poisonous. Asare, the youngest of the seven, possessed a lucky arrow with which he managed to hunt a few small lizards. This meagre food could not feed all seven of them.

Craving water, the eldest brother pointed to the tucum nuts which contained a sweet liquid which would stave their thirst. But it was not enough. The eldest brother pointed to a moist patch of soil. If we dig here, he told his brothers, we will find a spring. So they dug and dug and dug. Suddenly a huge rush of water burst from the ground, filling the sky with a fountain. They drank and drank. The water became a stream. And the stream flowed to a river. And the river flowed to a lake which then became an ocean.

Asare rejoiced at the water but despaired of the small lizards which had been washed away by the river. Even worse, his lucky arrow was now on the other side of the river. Without hesitation, he dived into the river despite the fact that he was unable to swim. He grabbed onto a floating log only to find it was not the benign piece of wood he expected.

A new animal had been created by the magic river from the small lizards it had swept away. This large, black animal was the first alligator. Asare asked the beast if he could climb on its back, but in doing so he addressed him as Mr Ugly Long Nose. The alligator did not like such a name, and snapped at Asare with his wide jaws and sharp teeth. Asare discovered he could swim after all. He swam very fast to the dry river bank with the alligator very close behind.

He begged the woodpeckers for help and they showered him with bark which hid his body and disguised his smell from the angry alligator. The alligator took him for a strange monster. Asare told the alligator the human had run into the forest and pointed in the direction the alligator should follow. The woodpeckers laughed loud. The monkeys who saw the muddy, bark-covered Asare laughed loud, but pointed to a pile of jatoba fruit skins they had discarded. Asare hid in the skins.

The alligator asked the monkeys if they had seen the human. They laughed out loud. The alligator knew that monkeys were silly creatures and he would get no sense from them, so he returned to his river defeated. After many adventures, Asare found his brothers who rejoiced in finding him still alive.

The brothers bathed in the new ocean. Their shiny clean bodies can now be seen in the sky as stars, as a constellation still known as the Seven Brothers.

South America is also the home of the broad-nosed caiman (*Caiman latirostris*). It is found in southern Brazil, through Uruguay and then west, to Argentina, Paraguay and Bolivia. It is an adaptable species, being found in swamps, mangroves and marshes, as well as man-made watering holes such as cattle stock ponds and dams. Its range overlaps that of the Yacaré caiman (*Caiman yacare*), although the latter is found mainly in swamps and mangroves.

One of the most endangered crocodilians in the world, the Orinoco crocodile (*Crocodylus intermedius*) can be found in very small numbers in Colombia and Venezuela. It is a large crocodile, with recorded specimens of 5 metres. There are reports of individuals reaching as much as 7 metres in length but none of these, or reports of Orinoco crocodiles attacking humans, have been confirmed.

Many South and Central American tribes worship crocodilian gods, who are generally associated with fertility and death. The Mayan god Ah Puch took a crocodilian form, and Mayan art portrays crocodiles alongside fields of crops and surrounded by waterlilies and fish. The Mayans also believed that a giant crocodile carried the world on its back, as it swam perpetually in a vast body of water. The region of Guatemala where most Mayan ruins have been found is home not only to the common caiman but also to two species of crocodile, Morelet's crocodile (*Crocodylus moreletii*) and the American crocodile (*Crocodylus acutus*). None of these species are dangerous to humans, so it is not surprising that their mythology revolves around fertility and food.

The Aztecs also worshipped a crocodilian fertility god, Cipactli, who looked after the crops. There is an Aztec creation myth which tells of the great earth monster, Tlaltecuhtli, who sometimes merges with another earth monster, described as a great caiman.

The gods who created the heavens and the earth were Quetzalcoatl and Tezcatlipoca. Descending from the sky, they observed Tlaltecuhtli striding across the sea. She had a fierce desire for flesh. Her gnashing teeth were not only in her jaw, but also in her knees and other joints. With such a horror present, Quetzalcoatl and Tezcatlipoca could not create the earth. Becoming two great serpents, they each seized a hand and foot of Tlaltecuhtli, tearing her apart. The ridges of her back became the mountains of the earth, while the rest of her body was tossed skyward to become the heavens.

Her violent slaying caused the other gods to be angry. They decreed that her body must be the source of all plants upon which humans depend. Trees and flowers would come from her hair, the smaller grasses and low plants from her skin. Wells, springs and small caves arose from her eyes, while her mouth provided great rivers and caverns. Hills and valleys derived from her snout.

The earth goddess was heard screaming for the blood of people, requiring the sacrificial heart and flesh to quell her rage. Without these, she would not continue to provide the nourishment essential for life.

The American crocodile is one of the larger crocodiles, with males commonly reaching 5 metres in length. It favours freshwater rivers, lakes and reservoirs and can be found in most of the northern countries of South America through to Central America, the southern states of the United States and the islands in the surrounding seas. It is an adaptable species that will also thrive in the brackish water of coastal regions. In the Dominican Republic there is a large population which lives in a totally land-locked salt lake, Lago Enriquillo. Another population lives in the cooling canals of the Turkey Point nuclear power plant in Florida. The American crocodile is also found on the Cayman Islands. Originally named Las Tortugas by Christopher Columbus because of their resemblance to two turtles, the islands' present name—the Caribbean for 'crocodile'—reflects their crocodilian inhabitants.

Morelet's crocodile lives in the freshwater swamps and marshes of Belize, Guatemala and Mexico. As we shall see in chapters 3 and 8, different species of crocodiles and alligators have different types of skin, some being more desirable to hunters than others. Unfortunately for the Morelet's crocodile, its skin is extremely desirable, and its numbers have been severely depleted by indiscriminate hunting.

The Cuban crocodile (*Crocodylus rhombifer*) is found only in a small area of Cuba, the Zapata Swamp. This is a medium-sized crocodile, with males reaching an average length of 3.5 metres. The Cuban crocodile is very partial to turtles, and has broader teeth at the back of its mouth than most other crocodiles to enable it to crush the shells of its prey. It is more agile on land than most other crocodiles and is a great leaper, using an underwater thrust from its long tail to propel it into the air. It is not known why the Cuban crocodile is so restricted in range, but this restriction means that they are in real danger of extinction.

How far into North America can we travel and still find crocodilians? Alligators will tolerate lower temperatures than crocodiles, but still prefer temperatures between 25°C and 32°C. The urban myth of a colony of alligators in the sewers of New York is just that, a myth. The American alligator (*Alligator mississippiensis*) is found in the south-eastern states, from North Carolina to Florida along the East Coast, and inland to Oklahoma and Texas. The American alligator is a large crocodilian, with the largest authenticated specimen, 'Old Monsurat', measuring in at 5.6 metres long. Killed in Louisiana in 1890, Old Monsurat had lost most of his teeth, which were no longer being replaced because of his age. He was probably about fifty years old.

Despite its reputation, the American alligator is naturally shy, even timid, unlike the aggressive saltie or Nile crocodile. However, as humans have moved into their habitats and even started feeding them, the alligators have become more aggressive. The alligator's natural diet is fish, augmented by turtles, birds, snakes, crabs and small mammals. As its waterways become more and more desirable residences for human populations, it is not surprising that the alligator has expanded its diet to include pet dogs and has even attacked humans.

The myth of the fearsome American alligator probably goes back to the early explorers of the New World. American naturalist William Bartram explored much of south-eastern America and reported seeing huge alligators which roared and blew clouds of smoke from their nostrils. He must have seen American alligators, who bellow in their misty swamps, but the imagery of an American dragon blowing smoke would have made for a much better story.

Both Native American and African-American folklores tell stories of the alligator and his tricky adversary, the rabbit, reminiscent of the Indian stories of the gharial and the monkey. The African-American version features that traditional trickster, Brer Rabbit.

Brer Alligator's back used to be smooth and white. He would climb from the water and lie in the sun, his white skin shining like silver. He was very proud of that skin. One hot day he was lying on a rice field bank, sunning his beautiful skin, when along came Brer Rabbit, who had no great love for Brer Alligator. Brer Rabbit stopped for a talk, because he was very fond of talking. He asked about the family, but Brer Alligator didn't reply. This annoyed Brer Rabbit, who said, 'We sure have been seeing a lot of trouble up here lately.' Brer Alligator said he'd never heard of Trouble and asked who he was. Being mischievous, Brer Rabbit decided to teach Brer Alligator a lesson. Brer Alligator asked to be taken to meet Trouble, but the more he begged and threatened, the more Brer Rabbit made excuses. Eventually he agreed to take Brer Alligator to meet Trouble the following Saturday.

As he prepared to meet Brer Rabbit early on the Saturday morning, Sister Alligator begged to come too. Then the young alligators insisted they come as well. They fixed themselves up with mud on their heads, marsh on their backs, and moonshine on their tails. They were very proud of how fine they looked. Brer Rabbit arrived, delighted he now had a whole family to trick, and amused by their ugly clothes of mud and marsh. Brer Rabbit and Brer 'Gator led, with Sister Alligator walking behind to make the little alligators behave, which they didn't. Brer Rabbit led them up the hill until he came to a field of broomgrass and briar. There he pretended to hear someone calling him, and told the alligators to wait. He laughed as he ran, grabbing a bunch of long, dry broomgrass. With a match from his pocket, he lit the broomgrass, blowing on it till it was well alight. He ran along the edge of the field and set it ablaze. Then he fled.

The wind caught the fire which flared high, the sparks and flames flying way up in the sky. The little alligators thought it was Trouble and that Trouble was pretty. Then the hot sparks started to land on their backs, first the little ones and then the adults. They cried out that Trouble hurts. Calling for Brer Rabbit, they ran around and around to escape the flames. When they could stand the flames no more, they ran back through the field, past Brer Rabbit, to the safety of the water. Brer Rabbit called to the fleeing alligators that they should never seek Trouble again. When they reached the safety of their water, they found their beautiful white skin was black and blistered, crinkled as a burnt log and rough as the oak. And that is why the alligator has a horny hide.

In common with many other indigenous peoples, Native Americans have totems that are central to their culture. A totem can be the symbol of a tribe, a family or an individual, and totem animals are respected as guides both through life and in the spirit world. The alligator totem represents maternal love, revenge, quickness and aggression, and it also stands for strong survival instincts, all of which are characteristic of the crocodilians. The Native American Choctaw legend of the Hunter and the Alligator not only draws on observed alligator behaviour, but also offers advice on sustaining the deer population by controlled hunting.

Once there was a hunter who never succeeded in bringing home a deer despite being the strongest man in the village. A jay would call and the deer would take flight or he would step on dry leaves and warn the deer or his arrow would glance off a branch and miss its target.

One day, deciding he would go deep into the swamps where there were many deer, the luckless hunter vowed he would not return empty-handed, even if he lost his life in the hunt. For three days he hunted without success. At noon on the fourth day, he came to a place in the swamp where a deep pool had dried out over the hot summer. On the sand was a huge alligator. It had been without water for many days and was close to death. The hunter's luck had been bad, but he knew that the alligator's was even worse. The hunter spoke to the alligator of his pity for him. The alligator's voice was so weak the hunter could barely hear it. 'Is there water nearby?' it asked.

The hunter told the alligator of a pond of water nearby which was fresh and cool and would not dry up. The alligator was too weak to travel there. He asked the hunter to come close. Despite his great fear of the alligator, the hunter did as he was asked. The alligator said, 'I know that you are a hunter and that you cannot kill the deer. If you help me, I will make you a great hunter.' The hunter was still wary, so asked that he might bind the jaws and legs of the alligator to take it to the waterhole. The alligator rolled over and allowed itself to be bound.

Using his great strength, the hunter carried the huge alligator to the water where he untied its feet. He untied the alligator's jaws, but held them together with one hand. Then he jumped back quickly. The alligator rolled over and dived into the deep water. It stayed under then rose, dived and rose and then dived a third time. Staying under even longer, it finally returned to speak to the hunter who had been waiting on a high bank. The alligator thanked the man and told him how to become a great hunter: 'Go into the woods with your bow and arrows. There you will meet a small doe, still too young to have young of her own. Greet but do not kill that deer. Your power will increase. Then you will meet a large doe who has fawns and will have for many more years. Greet but do not kill her either. Your power will increase even more. Next you will meet a small buck who will father many young. Greet but do not kill the buck and your power will increase yet again. Finally you will meet a large buck, an old buck who has served his purpose. Take that buck and be grateful for his sacrifice. Follow my instructions and you will be the greatest of hunters.'

Doing exactly as the alligator had bid him, the man became the greatest hunter in his village. That is why the Choctaws became great hunters of the deer. By following the alligator's teachings, there were always deer for them to hunt.

On our travels around the habitats of the world's crocodilians we have seen many variations on similar themes, but one that stands out is the respect, even veneration, with which these great beasts are regarded by the indigenous peoples who share their habitats. Despite this, some species of crocodilians have been hunted to extinction and others are in imminent danger of extinction in the wild. However, the crocodilians' only 'natural' predator is man. When we consider their physiology and behaviour in more detail, it becomes obvious why they are the lords of all they survey.

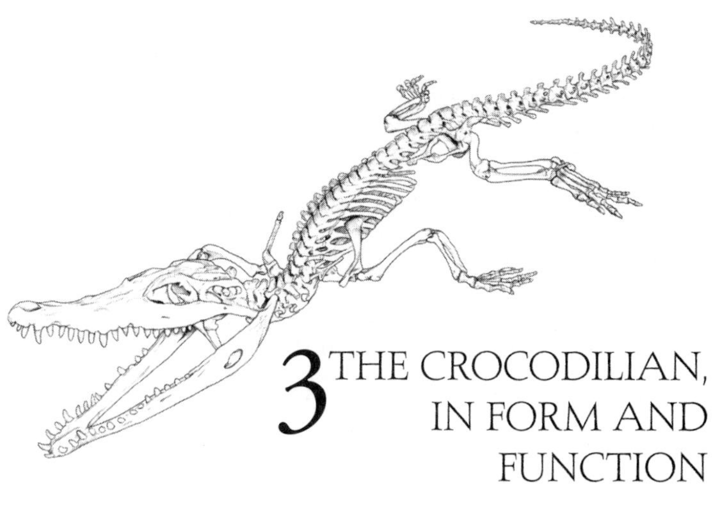

3 THE CROCODILIAN, IN FORM AND FUNCTION

Consider the chief of beasts, the crocodile who devours cattle
as they were grass.
What strength is his loins. What power in the muscles of
his belly.
His tail is as rigid as a cedar, the sinews of his flanks are
closely knit.
His bones are like tubes of bronze, and his limbs like bars
of iron.
He is the chief of God's works, made to be a tyrant over
his peers,
for he takes the animals of the hills for his prey and in his jaws
he crushes all the wild beasts.

There under the lotus plants he lies hidden in the reeds and the marsh.
The lotus flower conceals him in its shadow.

This description from the Book of Job portrays an awesome beast. Many people immediately associate crocodiles with enormous jaws and fearsome teeth. The muscles in crocodilian jaws make them capable of enormous power, and large crocodilians can crush turtle shells or the skulls of their prey in a single movement. The American alligator has the highest bite-force for its size of any crocodilian, and the saltwater and Nile crocodiles have the highest of any living animal.

However, most of the crocodilian's power is contained in the downward movement, and the massive jaws can be contained by a strong rubber band. While it is relatively easy to keep a crocodilian's jaws closed, it's a different matter to try and open them. If a large crocodile doesn't want to open its mouth, it will take three or four people armed with levers to persuade it.

All crocodilians have the ability to regulate the salt and water balance in their bodies. This is called osmoregulation. They excrete excess salt in their urine and faeces, by respiration and through their skin. Intriguingly, some crocodiles and gharials have a salt gland on their tongues through which they also excrete excess salt. This allows them to tolerate salt water for longer periods. Without this gland, alligators and caimans don't seem to have the same ability and so are rarely found out of freshwater environments.

While his captors are perhaps not game enough to test the rubber-band theory, the enormous jaws of this Australian saltwater crocodile are nevertheless easily restrained with rope. (Courtesy Adam Britton)

Crocodilian jaws are used not only to dispatch prey, but also to sense it. Dotted along the upper and lower jaws of all crocodilians are small pits and dark speckles, sensory organs that can detect the slightest change in the pressure of the water around them so when their prey moves, they know. Crocodiles also have sensory organs all over their bodies.

Crocodilians' eyes are highly evolved to suit their role as predators. Placed very close together on the top of the head, they give excellent binocular vision enabling the crocodile to judge the position of its prey with precision. The protruding eyes rest just above the surface of the water while the submerged crocodile lies in wait, but they are retractable and can be drawn back into the eye sockets at the first sign of danger.

We have all heard of 'crocodile tears'. Is there such a thing? Well, yes. The crocodilian has three eyelids. The top and bottom lids are the normal, opaque eyelids found on most reptiles and mammals. A third, transparent eyelid moves sideways across the eye. This eyelid protects the otherwise 'open' eyes when the crocodilian submerges and attacks under water. The third eyelid also conceals the liquid excretions produced by the crocodilian tear glands. These saltwater 'tears' lubricate and clean the eye, and are not usually visible. However, if the crocodilian is out of the water for any length of time, the resulting dryness in its eyes will cause visible tears to be formed. This is possibly why both factual and fictional accounts tell of crocodiles weeping over their prey on a river bank.

Although the crocodile's eyesight under water is probably poor, it is better to have some vision rather than none. The light receptors in crocodilians' eyes include both cones and numerous rods, so it is assumed all crocodilians can see colours. Research has shown that some definitely can.

A crocodilian's pupil can close to a narrow, slit-like aperture in bright light, while opening to a full, circular pupil to allow maximum light collection in the dark. Crocodilians share this feature with other nocturnal reptiles and mammals. It means they can hunt both during the day and at night, though they tend to hunt mostly at night and in the dim light of dawn and dusk. Bright sunlight means that it is time for basking on the river bank.

Those who look for crocodilians at night know that it isn't hard to find them. Their eyes reflect the light of torches or spotlights for hundreds of metres. This is the result of an

An American alligator hatchling with its bottom eyelid closed. (Courtesy Damian Kelly)

additional layer of crystals behind the retina at the back of the eye, present in many animals. This layer is known as the *tapetum lucidum*, and the crystals reflect the light that passes through the retina back onto the retina, thus intensifying the image in low light.

Crocodilians have a very slow metabolic rate, compared to the rapid mammalian digestive system. The metabolic rate is influenced by temperature, and if a crocodile eats and become too cool to digest its food properly, the food may in fact rot in its stomach before it is completely digested. However, this is why wild crocodiles lose interest in food when the temperature falls. Crocodilians expend a large amount of energy killing their prey, large chunks of which are swallowed whole and then digested in their entirety. The crocodilian's stomach is relatively small for its size, so the crocodile has to rest and digest after each kill. It's never safe to assume, however, that the crocodile basking on the river bank has just eaten and therefore isn't dangerous. Crocodilians have also been observed to gorge in times of plenty and build up extra fat stores, particularly before the onset of the colder months.

Crocodilians eat less in the winter months, and the Australian freshwater crocodile eats very little during the dry season. Research indicates alligators don't eat at all during their winter hibernation.

Crocodilian stomachs are extremely acidic which facilitates the digestion process. Turtle and tortoise shells slowly dissolve, as do the bones of birds and mammals. After they have reached twelve months of age, all crocodilians begin to ingest stones known as gastroliths to aid the digestion process—John Lort Stokes noted the presence of 'fourteen pounds of pebbles, some of them measuring four inches in diameter' in the stomach of the 'alligator' he shot. It was originally thought by scientists that these gastroliths might act in the same way as a ship's ballast, to aid the crocodilian's stability in the water, but it is now more generally accepted that they are part of the digestive system. Crocodilians have been known to travel considerable distances in the hunt for suitable stones. If they can't find stones, they will ingest other solid objects such as coins or bottles, even zoologists' radio transmitters. Perhaps this is why so much jewellery has been found in the stomachs of the Indian gharials and muggers—jewellery worn by the dead on their final voyage down the Ganges.

Helpman described the Australian saltwater crocodiles as lying in wait for easy prey. Not all crocodilians feed on live mammals caught by the silent, rapid attacks we are so familiar with from nature programs. Some caimans are very successful bottom-feeders, using their broad snouts to scour the mud for mussels and other fauna. Most crocodilian species will eat carrion, and some will hunt as a pack.

Many crocodilians store food. The Nile crocodile (*Crocodylus niloticus*) will store a carcass under water to soften it, and it has been observed wedging its prey into branches to allow chunks to be torn from it. Sometimes a group of Nile crocodiles will take hold of the same carcass and thrash their bodies around in a twisting motion. This allows each to eat their fill. The Nile crocodile is one of the most successful crocodilian species, and it may be that this cooperative behaviour has contributed to that success. Groups of Nile crocodiles have been reported using their bodies and tails to corral a school of fish into the shallows, and thus gain an easy feed, although the dominant animals always feed first. They will also scavenge as a group for carrion on land.

Some crocodilians are more comfortable than others on dry land, but most are clumsy and ungainly out of the water. When we consider their physical structure, it's not surprising. The limbs, both in length and musculature, are relatively small compared to the length and weight of the crocodilian. The front limbs have minimal or no webbing, with five fingers. The rear limbs have four webbed toes, the inner three of which possess claws. A fourth large toe, also webbed but without a claw, and a rudimentary fifth complete the set. The animal's real power is in its tail, which consists of roughly half its body length.

The limbs play little to no part in swimming, and are held close to the body at higher speeds. From the neck to the point of the tail, the crocodilian undulates in a smooth and efficient wave motion, as it moves gracefully through the water. When stationary, or moving slowly, the crocodilian may splay the hind limbs to stabilise or to help steer itself.

When a crocodilian lies in the water, wary and observant, its body is held well below the waterline, the limbs splayed and only the eyes and tip of the nose visible above the surface. This posture is adopted in very young animals as well.

I was sceptical when I read that crocodilians are so streamlined and skilled at moving through the water that even the largest of them can approach its prey without causing a ripple. On a visit to the Australian Reptile Park, I stopped at a swamp populated with American alligators (*Alligator mississippiensis*) and smugly pointed out to my companions the distinct wake visible behind the swimming alligators. I was soon to be silenced, however. A large alligator approached a heron. With only its eyes and nostrils showing, it advanced on the bird without any discernible disturbance of the water. Despite the stealthy approach, the heron detected it anyway and flew off. I had the distinct impression these were very well-fed alligators and that such an impressive swim was merely for show.

A crocodilian cannot stay under water indefinitely but, in normal situations, they will stay under for ten to fifteen minutes. They can dive for longer if they need to and experiments with American alligators have shown that they can survive under water for well over an hour. Lacking gills, how do crocodilians manage to spend so much time under water? Part of the answer is a beautifully simple piece of physiological engineering. All crocodilians have a valve at the back of their throat called the palatal valve. When a crocodilian dives this valve closes, stopping water getting into its throat, oesophagus and trachea. The valve is so effective that the crocodilian can open its mouth under water without drowning, unlike its unfortunate prey.

An Australian freshwater crocodile hatchling mastering the art of the stealthy approach, with only its eyes and the top of its nose visible above the waterline. (Courtesy Damian Kelly)

When under water and stationary, the crocodilian's heart rate drops to as low as two or three beats per minute and they expel most of the air from their lungs. Crocodilian blood has a remarkable capacity to release the oxygen it carries as it is needed. The blood itself has a unique chemistry that enables it to utilise more oxygen from a breath of air than any other animal.

Even more extraordinary is the crocodilian heart. It combines features of both mammalian and reptilian hearts and utilises each as required. Coupled with an extremely efficient circulatory system, the crocodilian heart enables the animal to exploit its oxygen supply to the full.

The reptilian heart has three chambers. Oxygenated blood travels into the heart from the lungs, and oxygen-exhausted

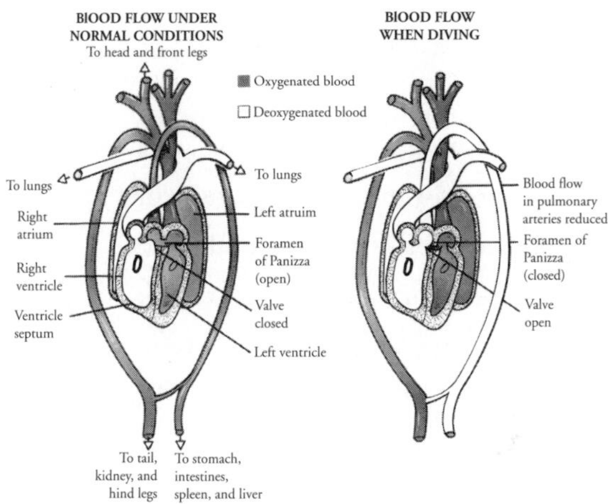

The crocodilian heart with its actively controlled muscular valves. (Reproduced with permission from Ross, 1989)

blood from the muscles and internal organs. The blood is mixed in a common ventricle and begins to circulate again. Not all blood that goes to the muscles and organs has been re-oxygenated, and some of the oxygenated blood returns to the lungs.

The crocodilian heart, however, has a partitioned ventricle so, in effect, has four chambers like a mammal. One side of the heart pumps blood to the lungs, the other pumps it around the body. The system becomes really impressive when the crocodilian submerges. If a crocodilian can't get fresh air into its lungs, it effectively disengages them. A unique valve, known as the foramen of panizza, closes off the lung circuit and redirects the blood to the vital organs. The crocodilian can control the flow so precisely that the blood goes directly to the brain and heart, where it is most needed. Crocodilians are the only animals that have actively controlled muscular valves in their hearts.

Once under water, the crocodilian can reduce the blood flow to its muscles, slow its heart rate to one or two beats per minute and wait in this resting mode until it needs to erupt into action. The beauty of the system can be seen in the speed with which the crocodile switches from an almost dormant state into one of full alert. Drawing breath as it suddenly rises, the crocodilian's heart is up to speed in seconds, and the full supply of energy-giving oxygen is being pumped out to its muscles.

Crocodilians do not have such sophisticated mechanisms to regulate their body temperature. All crocodilians are poikilothermic. This means that their internal body temperature depends primarily on their surrounding environment and that it is technically incorrect to refer to crocodilians as

American alligators alternating between the sun and the shallows to regulate their body temperature. (Courtesy Damian Kelly)

The familiar crocodile 'gape' pictured here is a behavioural posture, giving a warning that this animal has teeth and could do an intruder harm. It is also a crocodilian ventilation system, a way of keeping them cool. (Courtesy Damian Kelly)

cold-blooded. Because most crocodilians are only comfortable in tropical environments, their blood is rarely cold. The only crocodilians that can tolerate cooler temperatures are the American alligator and the Chinese alligator, both of whom hibernate through the coldest months of the year.

In the early Tertiary Period, more than 35 million years ago, crocodilian species flourished in North America and Europe. The later Tertiary Period, just before the Pleistocene Ice Age, saw the crocodilians retreating towards the equator before the advancing cold.

Crocodilians prefer to keep their body temperature between 30°C and 33°C, but they have no internal mechanism to keep them warm. They cannot shiver, and they have no insulation such as that offered by fur or feathers. They

The scutes (also known as osteoderms) of a young Australian saltwater crocodile. (Courtesy Damian Kelly)

maintain their body temperature by their behaviour. Water has a more constant temperature than land, but crocodilians bask in the sun to raise their body temperature. If they become too hot, they simply move to the shade or back into the water. They will also laze in river mud, which is warmer than surrounding water. In addition, the crocodilians have built-in solar panels on their backs. Infra-red cameras have shown that the scutes, or bony ridges, on their backs trap the sun's heat, giving the animals an extra source of warmth. The scutes are also known as osteoderms.

Poikilothermic creatures do not have to expend as much energy to keep themselves warm as the less energy efficient warm-blooded animals. They can store their surplus energy as fat, giving them resources to draw upon should food become scarce. Being poikilothermic, the fat stores last for extraordinarily long periods compared to mammals. If food is plentiful, however, crocodilians can grow surprisingly rapidly. Young crocodilians of the larger species can grow as much as 1 metre in their first year, although this growth rate slows dramatically as they approach adulthood. In general, a very large crocodile is a very old crocodile.

Agile and deadly in the water, how dangerous is a large crocodilian on land? There are many far-fetched and frightening tales of monster crocodiles running down their fleeing prey. John Lort Stokes described the crocodile he shot as getting up and 'running' after one of his crew. The truth is that crocodilians' forte is sudden attack rather than sustained pursuit, and most will flee rather than chase. True, a crocodile can reach speeds of 12 to 14 kilometres an hour, but only for short distances. Australian freshwater crocodiles trying to escape a threat have been recorded at 18 kilometres per hour for up to 30 metres, but then they tire. One hundred metres and they are exhausted. The urban myth is that to outrun a crocodile you should run in a zigzag fashion. Don't. You might take a zigzag path but the crocodile won't, and it'll close the distance between you. Run straight, run fast and you will outrun the crocodile. Don't look back.

Unlike other reptiles, crocodilians have more than one gait on land. On smooth surfaces such as mud flats, crocodilians belly crawl. In this they resemble lizards, using their legs to propel them along. Rapid leg movement and a swaying gait can lead to quite a fast pace which, again, is usually used for flight rather than pursuit. As a belly crawl is quite similar to the crocodile's swimming motion, it can lead to a seamless transition from land to water.

Over rougher terrain, crocodilians can high walk, bringing their legs directly underneath them in a much more mammalian way. It's not fast, or elegant, but it allows them to navigate rocky ground efficiently. And then there's the gallop. Yes, a real equine gallop. The front and back legs work in pairs, moving in sequence. A galloping crocodilian is something to see. Although all crocodilians can gallop, unsurprisingly it's more common in the smaller species. Only the Australian freshwater crocodile and the Cuban crocodile have ever been observed to use the gallop in attack.

Crocodilians are the most efficient predators in their ecosystems, and they guard their territories jealously. Saltwater

An Australian saltwater crocodile sliding down a muddy bank in a belly crawl. (Courtesy Adam Britton)

crocodiles are the most territorial of all crocodilians, and their territory in the wild can range from a few hundred metres to several kilometres in length. Both male and female adults will see off intruders. An adult female will often drive other females away from the nesting ground she has selected. She will defend her nest sites vigorously, going without food if necessary. As her eggs will take between seventy and ninety-five days to hatch, a nesting female can lose a lot of condition.

Dominant crocodilian males will not tolerate intruders in their territories. Battles commence with a series of displays and rituals. The dominant animal will raise its body out of the water, trying to intimidate its challenger. Submissive animals will raise their heads at a steep angle, offering their throats to the dominant male. They will sometimes also vocalise their submission. There is a huge range of sounds made by crocodilians, the most common being low growls produced by forcing air through the larynx. Should the intimidatory display fail, however, the dominant male becomes more intent on punishing the presumptuous intruder. Lifting its head and body from the water, the attacker smashes down onto the head or body of its opponent, often at an angle with jaws open. This crashing blow from a head solid with reinforced bone and jaws full of strong sharp teeth can do great damage. Bones are smashed, skin is ripped and teeth fly. Another strategy is to try and bite their opponent on the body, tail or limbs, occasionally holding on and spinning the body to inflict massive damage.

Two Australian saltwater crocodiles engaged in battle. Notice the attacker smashing down on his opponent. (Courtesy Adam Britton)

Despite the considerable damage that can be inflicted in these battles, the wounds are rarely fatal. The defeated crocodile moves aside and continues his search for a new territory. As we shall see in later chapters, this territorial behaviour is, to a certain extent, limited in captivity, but fights between adults of both sexes can still break out.

The wounds crocodilians inflict on each other would be fatal to a mammal, either through loss of blood or infection from the muddy water that is the crocodilian home. However, crocodilians have an incredible immune system, perhaps the most efficient of any animal. Even serious gashes can heal within a few days. It has only been recently discovered that they have an antibiotic in their blood, which has been named 'crocodillin'. Research is now being conducted to see how this knowledge may be used to benefit humans.

A crocodile can also grow new teeth to replace any knocked out in a fight. The teeth vary in size and shape to reflect their different functions. They only last a few years, and for only half that time are they exposed and functional. Successional teeth develop in a shallow pocket in the tooth socket, rising into an internal cavity within the functional tooth. As the young tooth reaches full size, the older crown falls away and the roots are reabsorbed. Front teeth

The front teeth of the crocodile are used for piercing and holding, and the back for crushing. (Courtesy Damian Kelly)

are replaced more frequently than back ones. This means that a crocodilian's jaw is full of teeth of various sizes, all constantly being replaced, until old age reduces the replacement regularity.

Crocodilian males fight not only for territory, but also for the right to impregnate the local females. All crocodilian species are polygamous, and the dominant male will mate with all the sexually mature females in his territory. The sexual maturity of crocodilians is quoted in body length not age, because growth rates depend on the resources available. The female saltwater crocodile reaches sexual maturity between 2.2 and 2.5 metres, and the male typically over 3 metres. This will usually take over ten years. The Australian freshwater crocodile also takes about ten years to mature, but the sign of sexual maturity is a length of about 1.4 metres. Some crocodilians mature faster than this. The common caiman, for example, takes between four and seven years to mature at 1.2 metres. The only reasonable way to estimate the age of a crocodile is to look at their bones. Like trees, they lay down growth rings. These not only indicate the number of years but also give some idea of the rate of growth in given years. Wetter years lead to more rapid growth. Inner rings can be obliterated, however, so the technique isn't absolute.

Mating behaviour varies between species, from the very formalised, predictable rituals of the American crocodile, to the fairly flexible rituals and unpredictable success in mating of the American alligator. Behaviour includes snout contact and lifting, head and body rubbing, body riding, circling and swimming displays. Given the size of the larger crocodilians, the actual act of mating takes place in the water.

Crocodilians have a much more acute sense of hearing than other reptiles, and sound plays a large part in the mating rituals of a number of crocodilian species. Crocodilian eardrums are on either side of the head and are protected by a flap of tissue. A continuous auditory canal connects both eardrums. American alligators bellow loudly during the courting and mating seasons. This bellowing can be so strong that the alligators vibrate along the entire length of their bodies. Once an individual starts, a whole group can bellow and vibrate in chorus—a truly alarming sound and sight for the unwary, but obviously intoxicating to those taking part. Other crocodilian males rumble, cough or bark to attract their females.

When a female saltwater crocodile has accepted a male's attention, the two will swim slowly side by side, bonding until the actual mating occurs. As the female arches her back to indicate submission, both her head and tail momentarily become submerged. The male will rub his head backwards and forwards across her neck and then mount her. He wraps his hind legs around her and his tail beneath her, so the undersides of the two are in contact. The vents (cloacas) are small openings at the base of the tail within which are the male's penis and the female's oviducts. The vents are aligned, allowing penetration and impregnation. Mating takes up to

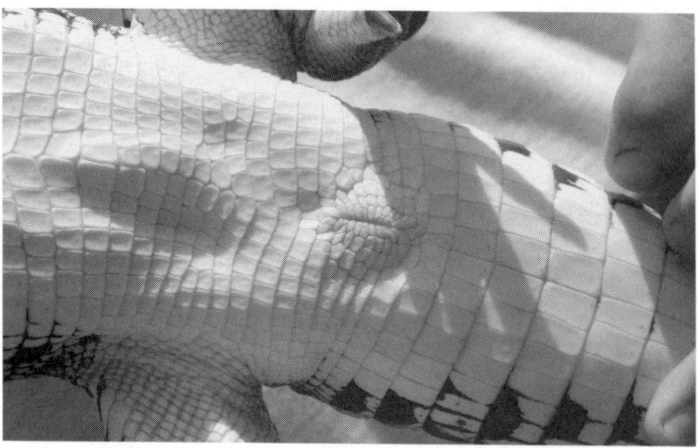

The vent (cloacas) of a young crocodile. (Courtesy Damian Kelly)

fifteen minutes and may happen only once or may be repeated. The mating pair may submerge and resurface frequently.

Although grown crocodiles have only two enemies, man and others of their own species, crocodilian hatchlings have at most 1 per cent chance of reaching maturity. Saltwater crocodiles construct their mound nests in the wet season, from November to March, thus running the risk of flooded nests. As the embryonic crocodiles breathe through their porous eggshells, a flooded nest means flooded eggs and no hatchlings.

Australian freshwater crocodiles are hole nesters and, unlike their territorial cousins, the females will often dig their holes within a metre of each other, if space is limited. All crocodilians nest in either mounds or holes, although some populations of the American crocodile switch nesting strategy depending on the situation. The American crocodile will also share her nest and, while she's not unique in this behaviour, the common caiman's cooperative nesting is. Typically, two or three common caiman females will lay their eggs in the same mound and guard them together. Perhaps this cooperative behaviour has come about as the result of the predation of the large predatory lizard, the tegu, which has been reported as destroying up to 80 per cent of the caimans' nests in its search for eggs.

The size of the female determines the number of eggs and their size. A larger, older female will produce more or larger eggs, or both. There is significant variation, however, both within and between species. Saltwater crocodiles, for example, lay between forty and sixty eggs in a clutch, while the freshwater crocodile clutch size is between four and twenty eggs.

Crocodilian eggs are not unlike bird's eggs, having an inner membrane and an outer, calcified shell. It takes between two and three months for the little crocodilians to be ready to hatch. To break out of the egg, hatchlings use what is called an 'egg tooth'. This is not actually a tooth, but a tough, horny piece of skin on the tip of the snout. It is not particularly sharp, but it helps cut through the egg membrane. The hatchling then uses its nose to break the outer shell. Within a few weeks, the egg tooth will break down and disappear.

The crocodilians' heightened sense of hearing now comes into play as the hatchlings call to their mother, who then uncovers the eggs within the nest. In a few species, the males will also help excavate the hatchlings. The vibrations this causes may stimulate some of the more reluctant hatchlings to break

American alligator hatchling. (Courtesy Damian Kelly)

out of their eggs. If some still show no sign of emerging, the female will take the egg in her powerful jaws, rolling and squeezing it between her tongue and the roof of her mouth. The shell breaks and the hatchling emerges, at around 20 to 30 centimetres in length, depending on species and conditions. Even the

Australian freshwater crocodile hatchlings. (Courtesy Damian Kelly)

largest crocodilian, with jaws capable of crushing a turtle's shell or a zebra's skull, can take her own egg and gently break it open without harming her young. Without their mother's intervention, these trapped babies would suffocate and die.

From the moment the tiny hatchlings break free of their eggs, they are capable of swimming and feeding. Their mother carries them to the river in her jaws, where she places them in the water for the first time. The baby crocodilians will stay close to their mothers in a pod or crèche, sometimes for months. Crocodilian mothers and their young communicate by grunting sounds before hatching. They continue to communicate in this way, sometimes for years. The hatchlings that make it to the water still face many dangers as their size leaves them vulnerable to attack from predators. Less than one in every hundred will make it to maturity. When they are still so small, they are very appealing food to birds, carnivorous mammals, large fish, turtles and even large frogs. Larger reptiles will also eat them, including their own kind. Many baby crocodiles are eaten by other crocodiles of the same species, even though the mother will try to defend them. This is a rather harsh form of population regulation. Not many young are needed if the area is well populated with adults. If it isn't, they have a better chance of survival.

As I hope is becoming clear, despite their wide range of territories and habitats, crocodilians display some marked family resemblances and character traits, as well as some species-specific behaviours.

But who studies the crocodilians, and how?

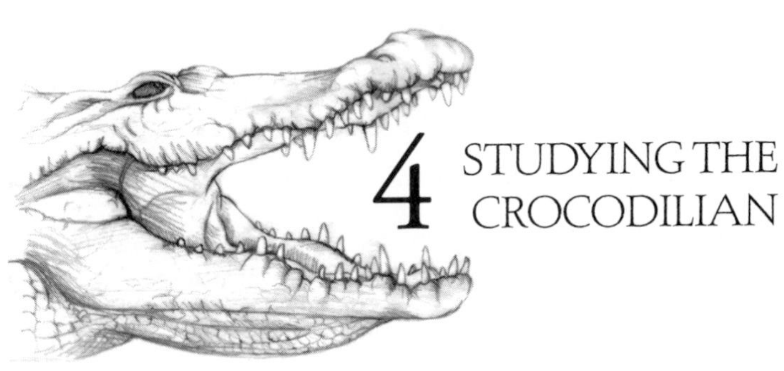

4 STUDYING THE CROCODILIAN

She had, the guide informed him later,
Been eaten by an alligator.
Professor Twist could not but smile.
'You mean,' he said, 'a crocodile.'

In his poem 'The Purist', Ogden Nash tells the story of Professor Twist, who has the misfortune to lose his bride while they are camped on a tropical river bank. Nash would no doubt agree with those who argue that scientists are purists. An alligator can never be a crocodile in the world of the zoologist. Zoologists and taxonomists define and classify, argue and re-classify, but who makes the decision on how to name and define a given species?

Taxonomy, the science which classifies all living things, takes its name from the Greek verb *kosmos*, to 'arrange'. Its founder, a Swedish botanist best known by his Latinised name, Carolus Linnaeus, first published his *Systema naturae* in 1735 and much of his system is still in use today.

Born in Sweden in 1707, from a very young age Linnaeus showed a fascination for naming plants in his father's garden. Although his family hoped that he would follow his father into the church, Linnaeus decided to study medicine at university. He spent most of his time collecting plants and, in 1735, while studying in the Netherlands, Linnaeus published the first edition of his classification of living things.

Linnaeus presented a new classification for the three kingdoms of nature recognised at the time: the animal kingdom, the plant kingdom and the kingdom of stones. The classification of the plant kingdom was new to science. Linnaeus classified the plants by grouping together those with the same number of stamens. Animals were also reorganised and, significantly, humans were for the first time placed with the monkeys. At only eleven pages in its first edition, *Systema naturae*'s importance far outweighed its extent. By 1770, the thirteenth edition contained 3000 pages. Linnaeus updated his groupings in each edition; for example, in the tenth edition he moved the whales from the fishes to the mammals.

Linnaeus first grouped similar species into a *genus*, from the Greek for 'race' or 'sort'. Groups of related genera were placed in an *order*. Similar orders were then placed in a *class*.

Only the first step in the process, establishing the species, is based purely on scientific evidence. From genus upwards, we are working with human constructs which are, by definition, subjective. So the debates on classification flourish.

The scientific name of any animal includes first its genus name and then its species name. The creature asleep on my lap as I type is a *Canis familiaris*. Technically, all domestic dog breeds can interbreed in the wild and produce fertile young, so all the different domestic dog breeds are considered one species, *Canis familiaris*. There are many members of that species, however, that would not fit comfortably on the lap of someone working at a computer.

Around 1800 French naturalist Georges Cuvier added a higher level of classification to Linnaeus's genus, order and class. The *phylum* contains animals of a similar body form and, thanks to Cuvier, the dog on my lap belongs to the same phylum as the crocodile, that of the vertebrates.

In 1758 Linnaeus named the common caiman *Caiman crocodilus* as part of his goal to create an encyclopaedic record of every species of plant and animal on earth. These were the days when species new to science were being named by the truckload. In 1758 alone, according to the Integrated Taxonomic Information System listing at www.itis.usda.gov, 2436 species were attributed to Linnaeus. Most are still valid. Over a thousand more are attributed to him in total.

Interestingly for his time, Linnaeus used what was considered almost erotic language in his descriptions: 'The flowers' leaves . . . serve as bridal beds which the Creator has so gloriously arranged, adorned with such noble bed curtains, and perfumed with so many soft scents that the bridegroom with his bride might there celebrate their nuptials with so much the greater solemnity . . .'

Linnaeus dealt with the most vocal of his critics in the most admirable way imaginable: he named insignificant or noxious weeds after them. Botanist Johann Siegesbeck labelled Linnaeus's sexually explicit language 'loathsome harlotry'. Linnaeus retaliated by naming a small, useless European weed *Siegesbeckia*.

We couldn't have a single book classifying our knowledge of species today—there are just too many of them. The systematic approach so well defined by Linnaeus still dominates biology. In particular, what survives of the Linnean system today is the basis of hierarchical classification and the consistent use of two words to name a species. Australia's two species of crocodiles can be identified precisely by using their scientific name thanks to Linnaeus and his successors.

As we saw in Chapter 1, the saltwater crocodile got its species name, *porosus*, from the Greek word for 'callus' because of the calluses found on their snouts. But what about *Crocodylus johnstoni*, the Australian freshwater crocodile?

In 1874 Gerard Krefft was dismissed in disgrace as Curator of the Australian Museum. This may have been in part because of his vigorous defence of the colonial expertise when it came to naming their own creatures. He enraged Sir Richard

Owen, Superintendent of the Natural History Departments of the British Museum, but not before he managed to get his name in the brackets after the scientific name of the Australian freshwater crocodile (*Crocodylus johnstoni* Krefft 1873). Krefft was not just a name in brackets but a real naturalist who, in 1873, formally classified the individual animal which he recognised as a new species.

In 1872, one Robert Arthur Johnstone of Rockhampton Bay in Queensland sent a crocodile to the Australian Museum in Sydney. The animal was not much more than 2 metres in length despite appearing to be mature, and the then Curator of the Museum, Gerard Krefft, proposed the animal as a new species. It was accepted practice to send Australian specimens to the British Museum for formal identification. Krefft photographed the animal and wrote to Dr John Edward Gray, asking him to contact the Royal Society and propose '*Crocodylus johnsoni*' as a new species. Unfortunately for Mr Johnstone, Krefft misspelled his name in the letter to Gray, and so eventually a non-existent Mr Johnson gained credit for the discovery.

Gray was the Keeper of the Department of Zoology at the British Museum from 1840 to 1874. As one of the major collections in the world, rivalled only by the French Muséum National d'Histoire Naturelle in Paris, the British Zoological Society and hugely influential Royal Society had worked with the British Museum to establish this as a key collection site for the classification of the world's species. The collection now runs to over 68 million items. Gray supported Krefft's claim, writing:

> Mr Krefft has just sent me the photograph of a Crocodile from Australia, which he has named *Crocodilus johnsoni,* with the request that I would communicate to the Society some observations upon it . . .
>
> In many respects the appearance of the animal, and the form of the beak, are much like (especially in the want of dilatation at the sides, and in the moderate breadth of the end) those of the African false gavial, *Mecistops cataphractus*; but it has well developed lateral cervical shields, which are wanting in all the African specimens I have hitherto observed; and one cannot understand how a West-African Crocodile can have been taken to or found in Australia.
>
> Judging from the photograph, I believe it to be a new species of Crocodile; and the form, as far as I know, is peculiar to Australia.

Just to prevent confusion, Gray was referring to what we now call the slender-snouted crocodile (*Crocodylus cataphractus*), not the false gharial (*Tomistoma schlegelii*). As more is learned about different species they are often reclassified, hence the species, genus and even family can change as zoologists and taxonomists debate each creature.

Krefft later corrected the spelling of Johnstone's name, but the rules of the International Commission on Zoological

Nomenclature (ICZN) are applied rigorously. This body was founded in 1895 to regulate a uniform system of zoological nomenclature ensuring that every species of animal has a unique and universally accepted scientific name. The ICZN is now based at the Natural History Museum in London. Members of the Commission are elected by zoologists.

So the Australian freshwater crocodile's official name remains *Crocodylus johnsoni* (Krefft 1873) as was cited in the original publication. However most technical and non-technical publications spell the name as it was intended to be and, indeed, should be spelled—*Crocodylus johnstoni*. Robert Johnstone's crocodile still resides in the Australian Museum in Sydney, as the 'type' specimen for the Australian freshwater crocodile. The type specimen of an animal is the one with which all others purporting to be from the same species must be compared.

Every species has in brackets after it, the name of the person who first identified the type specimen as a new species. Gerard Krefft's name is now forever associated with the Australian freshwater crocodile, but who was he? A naturalist, yes, and a curator of the Australian Museum, but perhaps the only museum official ever accused of trafficking in obscene photographs and removed bodily from his museum by two prize fighters! Born in Germany in 1830, Krefft was a talented naturalist who was less skillful in interpersonal matters. As curator from 1861 to 1874, he antagonised most of the museum's Board of Directors. He was accused of mismanagement, if not personal involvement, when the staff taxonomist and his brother were found selling indecent photographs. The resulting scandal threatened to engulf Krefft. He refused to resign.

On 21 September 1874 one of the Trustees, Mr E. Hill, went to the Sydney Horse Bazaar and hired two prize fighters. Together they broke into Krefft's private apartments in the museum where they found him sitting in an armchair reading a book. Krefft, his chair and his book were summarily ejected onto the street. Krefft successfully sued Hill for damages, but he was not reinstated. The two scientists on the board, both previous curators of the museum, resigned in protest at his treatment. One wonders if the fact that the Australian freshwater crocodile will always be known as *Crocodylus johnstoni* (Krefft 1873) was of any consolation to Gerard Krefft.

It is generally accepted that there are twenty-three species of crocodilian living today, all of whom are members of the order *Crocodylia*, which consists of three families: *Crocodylidae*, *Alligatoridae* and *Gavialidae* (see Appendix 1 for a full list of species and how they are classified according to family, genus and species). The family *Crocodylidae* contains the fourteen 'true' crocodiles, including *Crocodylus porosus* and *Crocodylus johnstoni*. True crocodiles are distinguished by the fourth tooth in the lower jaw which is enlarged and prominent when the jaws are closed. The family *Alligatoridae* contains the alligators and the caimans. These have a much broader jaw. The fourth tooth fits into a notch in the broader upper jaw and so cannot be seen. The gharial, family *Gavialidae*, has a greatly elongated snout with a notch on the end. Just to confuse the issue, there is also the false gharial (*Tomistoma schlegelii*) with an elongated jaw, which is most commonly now classified as a true crocodile.

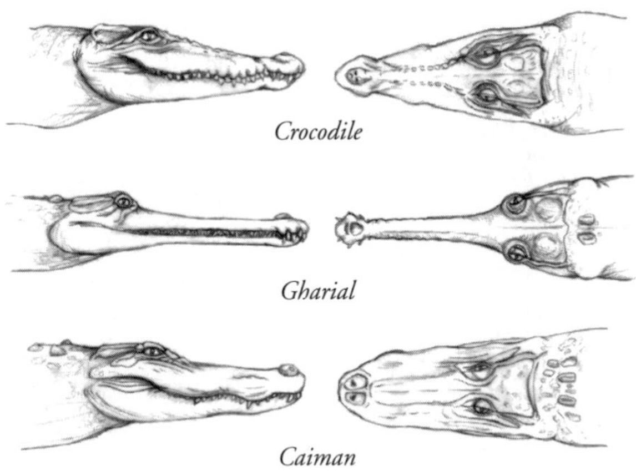

Crocodile

Gharial

Caiman

But what of *Caiman crocodilus*? When Linnaeus named the common caiman *Caiman crocodilus* in 1758, he included it in his blanket group of crocodilians, *Lacerta crocodilus.* The genus Caiman was first described by Johann Baptist von Spix in 1825. Ironically the correct classification for this species, one of the first crocodilians to be named, is still disputed. It has changed genus and species a number of times since 1758 as zoologists have debated its correct place. There are at least three, perhaps four, subspecies and it has as many as fourteen common names.

The common caiman, a subspecies of *Caiman crocodilus*, has many names: the spectacled caiman, Tinga, Baba, Babilla, Babiche, Cachirré, Caiman blanco, Caiman de Brasil, Cascarudo, Jacaretinga, Lagarto, Lagarto blanco and Yacaré blanco are all considered to be the same subspecies (*Caiman crocodilus crocodilus* or *C. c. crocodilus*). They are found in Columbia, Peru and parts of Brazil. Another generally accepted subspecies is the Rio Apaporis caiman (*C. c. apaporiensis*), which is found only in a 200-kilometre long stretch of the Apaporis River in south-east Columbia. The brown caiman (*C. c. fuscus*) is found across the north of South America and into Central America. It has also been introduced into Puerto Rico. Another subspecies is the Yacaré caiman (*C. c. yacare*), by which point things start to get pretty confusing. Two other subspecies (*C. c. paraguayensis* and *C. c. matogrossiensis*) have been suggested but rejected and the debate continues.

The debate continues to the point where the actual concept of a species is no longer clear-cut. The traditional definition of a species, as we saw with *Canis familiaris*, is a group of animals that can reproduce in the wild and produce fertile young. Most of the time, this definition holds, but zoologists know that fertile hybrids are becoming more and more common. Crocodilians are known to cross-breed in captive breeding programs and produce fertile young, but this does not mean the cross-breeding crocodilians are the same species. However, crocodilians are also now known to be cross-breeding in the wild, and two or more species can be hybridising along the overlap of their ranges. So the traditional definition doesn't hold up.

So what stops cross-breeding crocodilians being considered the same species? The difficulty is that currently there is no agreement within the field of exactly what a species is. Some biologists prefer the term 'taxonomic unit' for this reason. In different biological fields, they have different biases, the conservation biologists, for example, having different concerns to the evolutionary biologists.

Taxonomists define a species based on a range of criteria, including physical structure, behaviour, ecology and genetic make-up. Species are defined as being distinct if there is enough difference between the animals being compared. The fact that the traditional definition of a species is no longer watertight gives today's taxonomists and zoologists enormous scope to argue over the classification and reclassification of species. As Dr Adam Britton, zoologist and crocodile specialist, explained to me: 'If the old definition still held, we could just resolve these arguments by getting controversial animals to bonk each other and see what they produced down the line.

'To throw another spanner in the works, some croc farmers have been interbreeding hybrids for generations to try to improve growth rates—even triple hybrids (for example, *C. porosus* x *C. siamensis* x *C. rhombifer*) have been produced. They're as ugly as sin and God forbid any of them make it into the wild.'

The fact that there is still so much debate over the classification of the crocodilians is one reason they are so attractive to zoologists and naturalists. Another reason is that there is still so much we don't know about these animals. Scientists studying crocodiles today go way beyond simply classifying them. Adam Britton shared with me some of the fascination crocodiles hold for him.

As a young boy I become fascinated with dinosaurs, as many young boys do. The combination of large teeth, reptilian intelligence and monster size is irresistible. Compared with the relatively tame assemblage of fauna currently on the planet, the dinosaurs were truly astounding. I spent many hours travelling back in my own imaginative time machine to wander with these reptilian behemoths. It irrevocably affected my perception on the world.

I had one book on dinosaurs, and the last couple of pages had a profound effect on me—they talked about the crocodilians, which they described as the last living remnants of the dinosaurs. Of course we now know this isn't true—crocodilians are dinosaur cousins, not dinosaur descendants. But to a six-year-old eager to learn more, it was a bit of a revelation—living dinosaurs! Of course, they'd shrunk a bit, they no longer walked on two legs and made bellowing sounds that shook the very earth (or so I thought at the time!), and they didn't have cool names like *Tyrannosaurus* or *Deinonychus*, but they were the last living dinosaurs and I loved them! Dusty fossils be damned—here I could finally focus on living animals.

Since then I became secretly obsessed with crocodilians, and tried to figure out how I could achieve my dream of working with them as a career. As I went through school it was clear that I had a calling for science. For me, science was always about being a detective—trying to figure out how something worked, piecing together enough evidence so that you could prove a theory. Combining crocodiles and science naturally led me towards being a zoologist—a scientist who studies the natural world. Growing up in the UK, however, was not the ideal location for someone who was interested in large carnivorous reptiles. Crocodyliforms have been extinct in the UK for millions of years, and who could blame them—cold, miserable place that it is! So I always knew I'd have to travel overseas to achieve my goal. But first I had to educate myself.

Once I'd obtained my degree in zoology (which had absolutely zero crocodilian content!) I decided the pros outweighed the cons of doing a PhD. Trying to find a mentor who would tolerate my desire to study crocs proved impossible, however. I was on the verge of travelling overseas to study when I was offered an excellent opportunity to study bioacoustics in bats at the University of Bristol. Bats had long fascinated me, particularly their peculiar method of navigation using sonar.

Towards the end of my PhD, I was starting to get a bit

of a reputation. I was the guy who went into the library looking for journals containing bat research, and came out with a stack of journals containing crocodile research. I knew that completing my PhD would be the ticket I needed to finally enter the field of crocodile research. This was, I found, going to be a difficult proposition. After all, there aren't many people who want to study bats as a career, and there were actually even fewer people who wanted to actually do crocodile research as a career. Fortunately, after many trips overseas visiting crocodile farms, researchers and many wonderful people who encouraged me, I had a list of contacts—my secret list of people who I hoped would give me a job! One of these was Grahame Webb based in Darwin, Australia. I knew of Grahame from many years watching television shows featuring his work—the stuff of adventure and fantasy where people caught crocodiles at night with nothing but ropes, swooped around in helicopters over stunningly beautiful vistas, and generally lived the kind of life one can only dream about. I watched these shows over and over, wishing I could be there doing that. So when Grahame replied to my fax with a genial, 'No problem Adam, come over and volunteer for a year—we have a lot of crocodile surveys to do, and lots of data to analyse', I was on cloud ten.

A few months later my dream had come true—I was catching crocodiles at night, swooping over swamps in helicopters, and doing real science where I knew that every dot and

Dr Adam Britton, zoologist and crocodilian specialist, pictured here with a large Australian saltie. (Courtesy Adam Britton)

every number represented a crocodile! After a year, Grahame must have been sufficiently impressed because he offered me a full-time job. That whole period was the best time of my life, and proved to me that determination and hard work really can pay off. I spent over nine years working there as part of the core research team before setting up my own crocodile-centric business with my crocodile-tolerant wife!

One goal I've always had is to inspire others to take the same career risks that I have—not necessarily working on crocodilians, but at the very least to believe that you're capable of doing what you really want in life. I'm fortunate to have been in a position to do this, mainly through a website that I established in 1995 which has since become the number one site for information on crocodilians on the Internet. I've lost count of the thousands of emails I've had over the years from people who have been inspired to try and work on

> crocs, or in the field of zoology. Since I moved to Australia I've had the chance to appear regularly on television and in the media, which represents a unique opportunity for me to inspire others the way that I was inspired, by lighting that spark of curiosity and fascination. Once the spark is there, I hope to keep fanning the flames!

The modern zoologist's fascination with an animal can lead to many different avenues. Take the crocodilian immune system, for example. In Chapter 3 we saw that crocodilians can recover from injury in a way that no human can. Not only can they stop the flow of blood to an injured limb so that they do not bleed to death, but they are incredibly resistant to infection. Their wounds heal remarkably quickly and Adam Britton had the idea of looking for antibiotic properties in their blood. Working with the BBC Science Unit, Adam was part of the team that discovered a powerful, natural antibiotic in crocodilian blood, which team member Dr Gill Diamond called 'crocodillin'. At the time of writing the team were collaborating with Dr Mark Merchant at McNeese State University in Louisiana. Dr Merchant has been studying the immune system of American alligators, and his ongoing research indicates that the alligator serum is effective against a wide range of bacteria, viruses (including HIV) and fungi. With Britton's blood samples from Australian saltwater and freshwater crocodiles, it is hoped to further this research which holds real potential to benefit human medicine.

Drawing on the ever-increasing fossil record available to them, scientists can hypothesise and, in some cases prove, theories about human evolution from the evolution of completely unrelated species. Although by the end of his life he accepted that new species within a genus may have arisen after Creation as a result of hybridisation, Linnaeus would not have enjoyed the debate sparked by the theories of evolution. In the preface to a later edition of *Systema Naturae*, he wrote:

> *Creationis telluris est gloria Dei ex opere Naturae per Hominem solum.* The Earth's creation is the glory of God, as seen from the works of Nature by Man alone. The study of nature would reveal the Divine Order of God's creation, and it was the naturalist's task to construct a 'natural classification' that would reveal this Order in the universe.

Some nineteenth-century biologists and naturalists were more successful than others in reconciling the Creation with Darwin's theory of evolution. The dinosaurs' crocodilian cousins provided a superb continuous fossil record—evidence that the Darwinians grabbed with glee.

5 IN SEARCH OF THE ANCIENT

So from his shell on Delta's showerless isle
Bursts into life the monster of the Nile;
First in translucent lymph with cobweb-threads
The brain's fine floating tissue swells, and spreads;
Nerve after nerve the glistening spine descends,
The red heart dances, the aorta bends;
Through each new gland the purple current glides,
New veins meandering drink the refluent tides;
Edge over edge expands the hardening scale,
And sheaths his slimy skin in silver mail.
Erewhile, emerging from the brooding sand,

With tyger-paw he prints the brineless strand,
High on the flood with speckled bosom swims,
Helm'd with broad tail, and oar'd with giant limbs;
Rolls his fierce eye-balls, clasps his iron claws,
And champs with gnashing teeth his massy jaws;
Old Nilus sighs along his cane-crown'd shores,
And swarthy Memphis trembles and adores.

Erasmus Darwin (1731–1802)

Sir Richard Owen was a famous nineteenth-century biologist and superintendent of the Natural History Departments of the British Museum, and the author responsible for the following extract describing a dramatic scene of crocodilians roaming the south of Britain sixty-five million years ago.

> Had any human being existed [in Tertiary times] and traversed the land where now the south of Britain rises from the ocean, he might have witnessed the crocodile cleaving the waters of its native river with the velocity of an arrow, and ever and anon rearing its long and slender snout above the waves, and making the banks re-echo with the loud, sharp snappings of its formidably-armed jaws. He might have watched the deadly struggle between the crocodile and the palæothere, and have been himself warned by the hoarse and deep bellowings of the alligator from the dangerous vicinity of its retreat. Our fossil evidences supply us with ample

> materials for this most strange picture of the animal life of ancient Britain; and what adds to the singularity and interest of the restored tableau vivant is the fact that it could not now be presented in any part of the world. The same forms of crocodilian reptile, it is true, still exist; but the habitats of the crocodile and the alligator are wide asunder . . .
>
> Not one representative of the crocodilian order naturally exists in any part of Europe; yet every form of the order once flourished in close proximity to each other in a territory which now forms part of England.

Owen believed that the crocodilians that existed in his day were the same forms as those that coexisted with the dinosaurs, though he recognised that their habitats had become widely different from those of their ancestors. Today many palaeontologists take issue with those who believe that crocodilians, in their modern form, walked with the dinosaurs.

The earliest ancestor of the modern crocodilians, however, did indeed walk with the dinosaurs, but it was land-based and a very different creature to the modern crocodile. It was called *Protosuchus* and it can be traced back to the Late Triassic Period, or 220 million years ago. By about 190 million years ago, *Protosuchus* had evolved into *Mesosuchus*, whose fossil remains indicate that he was adapting to a more watery environment. Another hundred million years and the Mesosuchia were now the Eusuchia, water-based carnivores. The eusuchian fossil record from North America indicates two distinct families of eusuchians, probably the ancestors of the modern crocodiles and alligators.

Protosuchus and his descendants were part of a group of reptiles called the archosaurs, the so-called 'ruling reptiles'. This group also included the dinosaurs and the flying pterosaurs. They dominated the land throughout the Mesozoic era, from 245 to 65 million years ago. The crocodilians were the only 'ruling reptiles' to survive the ecological disaster that wiped out the dinosaurs. They went on to survive the inevitable competition that would have ensued with the rise of the mammals and endless climate and habitat changes. How much sadder is it, then, that some crocodilian species may not survive the threat posed by man's excessive hunting and wanton habitat destruction?

A question that intrigues palaeontologists is why were the crocodilians so successful? Opinion is still divided as to what, exactly, was the cause of the great extinction 65 million years ago. What we do know is that around 70 per cent of species on the planet were wiped out. But how and why did the remaining 30 per cent survive? A logical theory is that those species that survived are those which require less sunlight or food, but there are exceptions. Corals feed on algae, which needs sunlight. They are also very sensitive to temperature changes in the sea, yet they survived the great extinction.

Many more land species than water species disappeared, perhaps because of the protective qualities of water. Water not only protects life, it also helps preserve the fossil record of those who have died. It is not easy to become a fossil. It is estimated that over 99 per cent of species do not make it into the fossil record. Most return their trace elements and minerals to the earth, 'dust unto dust'. For a body to become fossilised, it is a huge advantage if it lies in or near the water. First it must be covered with sediment, which protects it from exposure to the oxygen in the air. Slowly, very slowly, the collagen fibres in the bones, and sometimes the soft tissue surrounding them, can be replaced by minerals from the surrounding sediment to form a fossil. Should the new fossil then survive millennia of erosion and violent earth movements and remain intact enough to be recognisable, it then has to be found. The fact that the ancestry of the crocodile can be traced from the present day right back to one of the earliest ages of the dinosaurs means that the crocodilian fossil record offers some enticing insights into the history of evolution.

Until recently, fossils firmly identified as eusuchian had been found only in Europe, North America and Africa. When Austalian palaeontologist Dr Steve Salisbury started his PhD in 1995, only a handful of Cretaceous crocodilian remains had been found in Australia, though there were some from Lightning Ridge that looked tantalisingly like eusuchian remains. At nearly 100 million years old, this would make them one of the oldest fossils of this type of crocodilian anywhere in the world.

When Dr Salisbury first decided to focus on the eusuchians for his doctoral research he asked himself:

Steve Salisbury with the skull of the Isisford crocodilian, April 2005. (Courtesy Steve Salisbury)

When and where did eusuchians first evolve? Why and how did they evolve from the plethora of other crocodilian groups that existed during the latter part of the Age of Dinosaurs? And why are they the only group of crocodilians to persist today? Why, like all the other suborders of crocodilians that existed during the Cretaceous, did they not also

> go the way of the dinosaurs? [See the geological time line on page 138 for a graphic representation of ages and periods, and the evolution of the crocodilian.]

Armed with his questions, Salisbury headed off to study the eusuchian fossils in Europe and North America. Returning briefly to Australia for a conference in 1998, he visited palaeontologist Ralph Molnar at the Queensland Museum. A local grazier had found some pieces of what he thought might be a fossilised crustacean, near the town of Isisford. Molnar's suspicion that the animal might be an Early Cretaceous crocodilian intrigued Salisbury.

It takes time and effort for fossils to become the beautifully mounted specimens we see in museums. Salisbury was presented with thirteen blocks of sandstone, and could catch only glimpses of the blocks' contents. He saw enough, however, to let him think that not only were these the best fossilised crocodilian remains ever found in Australia, but possibly an animal considerably more exciting than first thought—that it might, in fact, be a very, very early eusuchian. He wrote:

> At this stage, both of the new specimens [the Lightning Ridge and Isisford specimens] were still encased in several blocks of sandstone, and only small portions of their skeletons were visible. It was thus difficult to be certain about what they looked like. But having recently studied the

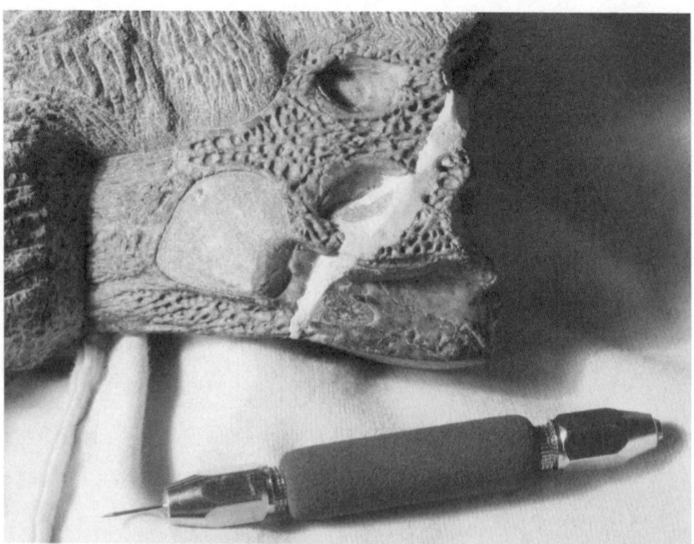

The skull of the Isisford crocodilian begins to emerge from its sandstone tomb in Steve Salisbury's lab at the University of Queensland, January 2005. The rock is carefully removed using Tungsten-carbide needles and hand-held pneumatic drills. (Courtesy Steve Salisbury)

material of *Bernissartia* [another eusuchian] in Belgium, I was confident that this crocodilian was something different. Importantly, the material appeared to show some of the characteristics of eusuchians. Was this the primitive eusuchian that the material from Lightning Ridge had been hinting at? I returned to Germany with the niggling feeling that the answer to all my questions lay in Australia after all. So commenced my association with the Isisford crocodilian.

Although neither specimen had been exposed, it was clear that they were both very well preserved. Breaks between the blocks indicated that the skeletons were articulated, with the bones preserved in close to what would have been

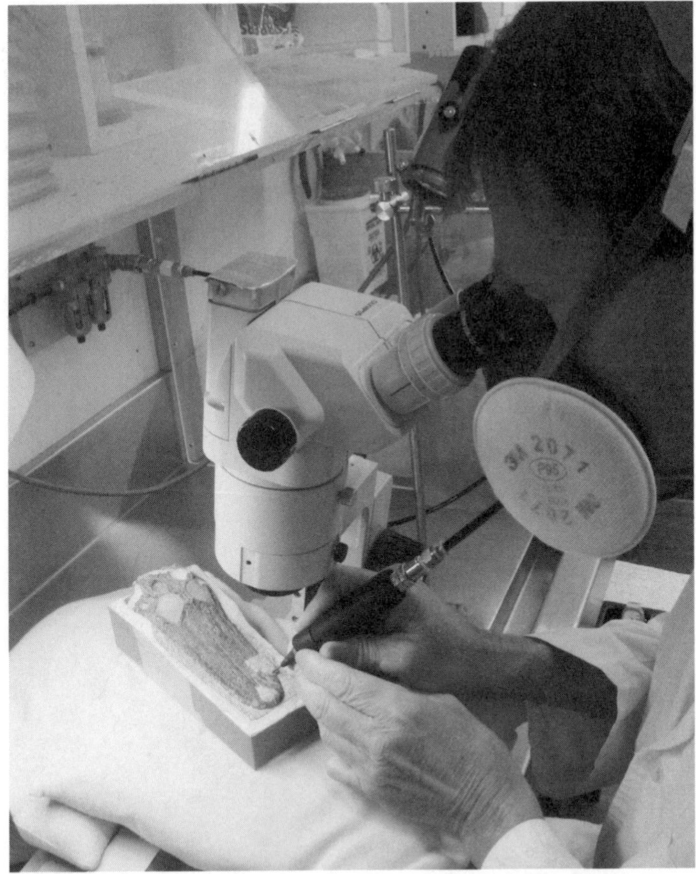

Kerry Geddes, the senior fossil preparator at the University of Queensland, carefully removes the final pieces of sandstone from the upper surface of the skull, April 2005. (Courtesy Steve Salisbury)

their position before the animal died. One of the specimens included portions of skull, neck, trunk and hind limbs, while the other was almost complete, with only the tail and part of the skull missing. Regardless of what type of crocodilian this material ended up being, it was clearly the best-preserved fossil crocodilian remains of any age yet found in Australia, and easily eclipsed any of the previously discovered Cretaceous material from Dinosaur Cove and Lightning Ridge.

Salisbury went back to Europe, where he spent the next eighteen months working with the fossil preparators at the State Museum of Natural History in Karlsruhe. Returning to Australia in 2000, he felt ready to start work guiding the team that would extract the fossils. Kerry Geddes, now Senior Technician in the Vertebrate Palaeontology Laboratory at the University of Queensland, spent his days armed with a diamond-bladed rock saw and a small pneumatic drill, chipping away at

Steve Salisbury sketching the completed upper surface of the skull of the Isisford crocodilian, April 2005. (Courtesy Steve Salisbury)

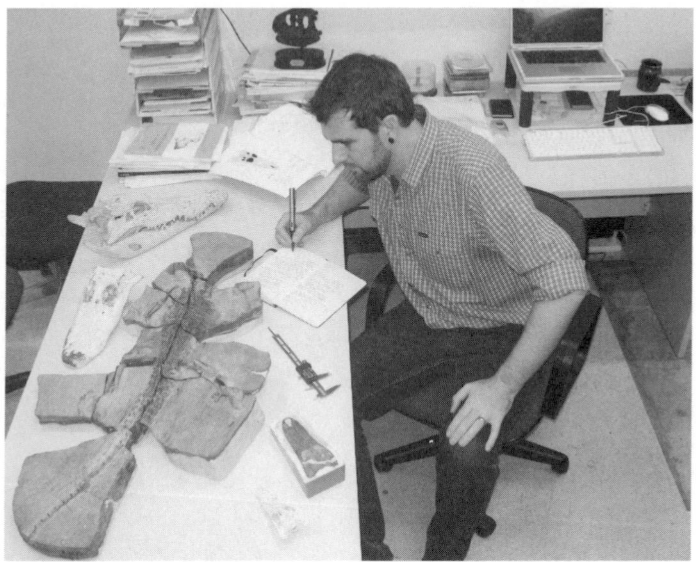

Steve Salisbury examining the skeleton of the Isisford crocodilian, April 2005. (Courtesy Steve Salisbury)

the protective rock. Two-and-a-half years would pass before he had fully exposed the fossilised remains.

In 2002, five years after he first saw the Isisford crocodile, Salisbury took a team out into the field to see if they could find the last portion of the fossil's tail. After ten frustrating days of drilling and digging, they uncovered the final bones.

The Isisford crocodile is the most complete crocodilian fossil ever discovered in Australia. Salisbury suspects that it is a new, and very primitive, eusuchian. At nearly 100 million years old, it predates the earliest known ancestors of the modern *Crocodylidae* by over 20 million years. As the best-preserved and most complete early eusuchian yet found anywhere in the

Matt Herne's reconstruction of the Isisford crocodilian, as it would have appeared 98–95 million years ago. As the world's first modern crocodilian, it shared its world with giant sauropod dinosaurs, and flat-footed herbivores known as orithopods. (Courtesy Matt Herne)

world, this now named specimen *Isisfordia duncani* has much to tell us about the first modern crocodilians.

The longevity of the crocodilians means that they play a crucial role not only in our understanding of evolution but also in the debate between evolutionists and creationists. While Benjamin Helpman was recording his first sights of the 'alligators' of north New Holland, the man who would become the *Beagle*'s most famous passenger was struggling with his conscience. After his three-year voyage on the *Beagle*, Charles Robert Darwin spent the next twenty years honing and refining the ideas that would eventually be published as the most radical new work of the nineteenth century. He knew that his theory of evolution as contained in *The Origin of Species* would deeply wound his devoutly religious wife, and cause a storm of protest. At fifty years old, he also worried whether he would be charged under England's laws of blasphemy and sedition.

A fiery young naturalist had no such qualms. Thomas Henry Huxley would become such a passionate advocate of evolution that he would be known as 'Darwin's Bulldog'. Although prepared to question some stages of the evolutionary process proposed by Darwin, Huxley would fight Darwin's battles on the public stage, amid the jeers and boos of incredulous audiences.

Huxley and Darwin's most implacable opponent was the foremost biologist of the time, Sir Richard Owen. The rift between science and the church captured the public imagination, filling public halls and newspaper columns. As fossils were unearthed, and models of dinosaurs and early crocodilians went on display in museums around the world, a new way of thinking was being forced on scientists and the public alike.

Despite his deserved reputation in scientific circles, and his genuinely ground-breaking work in identifying extinct animals, Owen had an unshakeable belief in the Creation. Coming from a comfortable background, and being well-educated at grammar school and university, Owen represented all that was conservative and respectable in the nineteenth century. Apprenticed to a local surgeon while still in his teens, Owen demonstrated the mania for collecting specimens that would become the hallmark of his brand of science.

> My zeal and skill at assisting at *post-mortems* had gained me the rarely bestowed commendation of the doctor our preceptor. I had already begun to form a small anatomical collection, and had lately added a human cranium to my series of the skulls of dogs and cats and the skeletons of mice and 'such small deer'. It happened also that on the day when a negro patient in the gaol hospital had died, a treatise on the 'Varieties of the Human Race' fell into my hands, and greatly increased my craniological longings. The examination of the body was over and the hurried inquest performed, when, slipping some silver into the hand of the old turnkey as we left the room, I told him I should have to call again that evening to look a little further into the matter, before the coffin was finally screwed down. It was but six weeks from the time of my first adventure in the old tower, when, provided with a strong brown-paper bag, I sallied forth on a fine frosty evening in January to secure my specimen of the

Ethiopian race. I was now an *habitué* of the place, and an attendant was no longer proffered to accompany me. Taking my lantern and keys, I opened every door and gate, duly locking them again after I had passed through. As I ascended the spiral stairs of Hadrian's Tower, speculations on 'facial angles,' 'prognathic jaws,' and that 'peculiar whiteness of the osseous tissue' upon which my favourite author had dilated, drove out of my head all the former broodings on immaterial beings which had so disturbed my first ascent of the tower. I particularly remember fastening after me the heavy door which led to the dark wide stone chamber of the dead, in order to be secure from any interruption in my work. The gloom of the apartment was just made visible by the light of the lantern, but it served for the business immediately in hand. The various instruments had judiciously been left behind; and when I returned through the gates—the bag under my cloak—the intimation that all was now ready for interment was received with a nod of intelligence by the old turnkey, which assured me that no inquisition nor discovery was to be apprehended on that side of the castle walls.

As soon as I was outside I began to hurry down the hill; but the pavement was coated with a thin sheet of ice, my foot slipped, and, being encumbered with my cloak, I lost my balance and fell forward with a shock which jerked the negro's head out of the bag, and sent it bounding down the slippery surface of the steep descent. As soon as I recovered my legs I raced desperately after it, but it was too late

> to arrest its progress. I saw it bounce against the door of a cottage facing the descent, which flew open and received me at the same time, as I was unable to stop my downward career. I heard shrieks, and saw the whisk of the garment of a female, who had rushed through the inner door; the room was empty; the ghastly head at my feet. I seized it and retreated, wrapping it in my cloak. I suppose I must have closed the door after me, but I never stopped till I reached the surgery.

Admitted to the Royal College of Surgeons in 1824, Owen was appointed Assistant Curator of the vast anatomical collection owned by John Hunter and housed in the College. By 1830 he had labelled, identified and catalogued each of the 13 000 animal specimens, and comparative anatomy had become his passion. The same year, he met the founder of vertebrate palaeontology, the French naturalist Georges Cuvier. In later years, Owen would delight in his nickname of 'the British Cuvier'.

Owen would be responsible for the formal descriptions of many of the specimens Darwin brought back from his voyage on the *Beagle*, and it was Owen's research on extinct birds and reptiles that led him to label these creatures 'dinosaurs' from the Greek words *deinos* 'terrible' and *sauros* 'lizard'. Despite this, his opposition to evolution would be his downfall.

In 1847 Owen was presented with a specimen of a new ape, the gorilla. Its superficial resemblance to man caught the public's imagination, but Owen was adamant that the gorilla's brain had no *hippocampus minor*, as found in the human brain. The human brain, therefore, was much more advanced than that of the gorilla. The one aspect of Darwin's mighty work on evolution that most enrages Creationists is his claim that we are descended from apes. Owen claimed that the gorilla's lack of a *hippocampus minor* proved that humans could not possibly be descended from such an inferior species. Unfortunately for Owen, his fiery young opponent, Thomas Huxley, would show that gorillas do, indeed, possess a *hippocampus minor*.

Twenty-one years younger than Owen, Huxley was from an educated but impoverished family and was almost entirely self-educated. His approach to natural history was in stark contrast to Owen's obsession with collecting and cataloguing specimens. Huxley would later say of Owen 'he is an able man, but to my mind not so great as he thinks himself. He can only work in the concrete from bone to bone, in abstract reasoning he becomes lost.' Like Owen, Huxley also attended a post mortem as a teenager, but experienced a very different reaction.

> The only part of my professional course which really and deeply interested me was Physiology, which is the mechanical engineering of living machines; and, notwithstanding that natural science has been my proper business, I am afraid there is very little of the genuine naturalist in me. I never

collected anything, and species work was always a burden to me; what I cared for was the architectural and engineering part of the business, the working out the wonderful unity of plan in the thousands and thousands of diverse living constructions, and the modifications of similar apparatuses to serve diverse ends. The extraordinary attraction I felt towards the study of the intricacies of living structure nearly proved fatal to me at the outset. I was a mere boy—I think between thirteen and fourteen years of age—when I was taken by some older student friends of mine to the first post-mortem examination I ever attended. All my life I have been most unfortunately sensitive to the disagreeables which attend anatomical pursuits; but on this occasion, my curiosity overpowered all other feelings, and I spent two or three hours in gratifying it. I did not cut myself, and none of the ordinary symptoms of dissection poison supervened, but poisoned I was somehow, and I remember sinking into a strange state of apathy.

Apprenticed to a doctor whose practice was in London's East End slums, Huxley was appalled at the degradation and privations he witnessed, and developed what would become a lifelong opposition to a Christianity he saw as failing the poor. Many years later he would coin the term 'agnostic' to describe his own belief system.

In search of a regular income, Huxley joined the Royal Navy and from 1846–50 served as assistant surgeon and naturalist aboard the *Rattlesnake* on her exploratory voyage of Australia and New Guinea. Huxley reported his discoveries as often as he could to the Linnaean Society, but he had no way of knowing how these reports were being received or, indeed, if they arrived at all. It was not until his return to England that he found out that not only had his reports on marine invertebrates been published, they had been very well received and his reputation as a scientist was assured. In 1851 Huxley's work was honoured by his election to the Royal Society, and the subsequent awarding of the society's Gold Medal.

As Huxley prepared to lock horns with Owen in the debate over evolution, he was already aware of Owen's vindictive nature towards other scientists. Gideon Mantell, a country obstetrician with an amateur interest in geology, was one to whom Owen showed particular malice. In 1822 Mantell found several large teeth which he was convinced were from the Mesozoic strata and therefore likely to be reptilian as at that time no mammal fossils had been found in that strata. Teeth are very important finds because their shape, composition and the way they fit into the jaw distinguish reptiles from mammals. Mantell believed that his teeth were from a reptile resembling the iguana, but twenty times larger, and so he named his find *Iguanodon* or 'iguana tooth'. Owen, however, was convinced that the teeth were mammalian. Georges Cuvier initially believed they came from a rhinoceros, but he later conceded they came from a herbivorous reptile. Mantell would be obsessed with *Iguanodon* for the remaining thirty years of his life. Eventually he acquired enough fossil evidence to show that *Iguanodon* would have been a biped, with its front limbs much smaller than its hind legs.

Mantell made his find at a time when fossils of large animals were being dug up due to an increase in mining, quarrying and agriculture. There was much excitement, for example, when a huge fossilised animal resembling a crocodile (later identified as an ichthyosaur) was discovered in Dorset. By 1853, the public's fascination with dinosaurs was such that Owen was asked to make a series of life-sized models for display in London's Crystal Palace. *Iguanodon* was to be the centrepiece. Owen ignored Mantell's thirty years of work and the 10-metre long model of the dinosaur was built with four thick stumpy, mammalian, feet. Mantell had died the year before, and Owen took all the credit for the discovery of *Iguanodon*.

Giant reptiles such as *Iguanodon* were changing the way people thought about God and his Creation. Although an outspoken opponent of Owen's Creationist views, Huxley had not yet fully accepted Darwin's theories on the gradual evolution of the species. He was convinced that Creationism no longer offered a viable explanation for the evidence encased in ancient rocks, but he still believed that a species could arise spontaneously and then remain unchanged. He did not agree with Darwin that natural selection, and a gradual evolution of traits which serve that selection, was the basis of the origin of species.

Darwin so respected Huxley's intellect and, no doubt, so appreciated his public support that he never gave up hope of converting Huxley to a full acceptance of his theories. It was only at the end of Huxley's career, after decades of defending evolution without being fully convinced of the details, that his complete conversion occurred—because of the crocodilians.

Huxley had been interested in the possible links between birds and reptiles for some time. He claimed that birds were an extremely modified reptilian type. He then linked the two in a vertebrate 'province' he called *Sauropsida*. Owen denied such a link, but Huxley stood firm. Dinosaurs, he proposed, had had bird-like hearts and may even have been hot-blooded.

In 1867 Huxley was still thinking that all living things were made according to a set of basic plans. This meant that reptiles and birds did not spring from the same ancestor but from the same plan. Then Huxley read Haeckel's *Morphologie* and underwent a profound change in his thinking. He had always told Darwin that the evolution of one species to another was not possible, but as he began to apply evolutionary theory to his understanding of birds he realised that not only was it possible, it was highly probable. In a condition of almost sustained hysteria, Huxley traced the evolution of birds back to a single ancestral line. Eight years after the publication of *The Origin of Species*, Huxley had come to terms with its most profound idea.

In autumn 1867 Huxley was at the Ashmolean Museum looking at the collection of *Megalosaurus* bones. As he studied the dinosaur's pelvic girdle more closely, he realised how avian the hipbones were in appearance. At that time a new dinosaur from America, *Hadrosaurus*, had been identified that was clearly bipedal. A different picture was starting to form, and Huxley was about to assign a dinosaur ancestry to the birds.

Huxley then went to the British Museum and began to reassemble the *Iguanodon* bones. The 5-metre tall herbivore became a biped, just as Mantell had always claimed. Huxley described it as 'a sort of cross between a crocodile and a kangaroo with a considerable touch of a bird about the pelvis and legs!'

On 7 February 1868 he addressed the Royal Institution, with his usual fire and panache:

> Those who hold the doctrine of Evolution, and I am one of them, believe that today's discrete classes of animal—including the birds and reptiles—have come from a common stock. But to find it we have to go back to a balmy Jurassic past, to a lagoon at Solnhofen. Flapping clumsily overhead was a heavy *Archaeopteryx.* And at the water's edge, a diminutive dinosaur, hopping like a bird, neck bobbing, snatching prey with its small arms.

Huxley had now publicly expressed his belief that different species could have common ancestors—that birds and dinosaurs came from the same stock. What he needed to do next was provide the proof, and he would find it in the crocodilians.

On 28 April 1875 Huxley's definitive paper was published in the *Quarterly Journal* of the Geological Society. In the discussion after its reading, the *Journal* noted, 'the case established by Prof. Huxley with regard to the Crocodiles furnished stronger support to the hypothesis than even that of *Hipparion* and the Horse'. This is how Huxley began his paper:

> Nearly seventeen years ago I had the honour of laying before the Geological Society an account of such remains of a remarkable reptile (*Stagonolepis Robertsoni*) as, up to that time, had been found in the sandstones of the neighbourhood of Elgin, and the conclusion at which I had arrived, 'that *Stagonolepis* is, in the main, a Crocodilian reptile' . . . From the evidence which has now been collected, and which consists entirely of specimens associated with the characteristic scutes of *Stagonolepis*, it is demonstrable that, in outward form, this reptile must have resembled one of the Caimans or Jacares of the present fauna of intertropical America, that it possessed strong limbs, of which the anterior were at least as large, in proportion to the posterior, as in the modern *Crocodilia*, but that *Stagonolepis* differed from the Caimans in possessing a long and narrow skull, more like that of a Gavial.

Huxley went on to list *Stagonolepis*'s similarities to the existing crocodilians, and also the differences in the numbers and arrangements of scutes, or bony ridges, on the animal's back. That this animal strongly resembled known crocodilians was indisputable. He wrote about the suborder *Eusuchia*, which did not become extinct and is the one that includes the living species. Huxley describes the eusuchians as 'the most Crocodilian of Crocodiles'. He wrote:

> Hence, if there is any valid historical foundation for the doctrine of evolution, the *Eusuchia* ought to have developed from the *Mesosuchia*, and these from the *Parasuchia*; and if this process of evolution had taken place under such conditions that the skeletons of *Crocodilia* which have been subject thereto have been preserved, geological evidence should show that the *Parasuchia* have proceeded the *Mesosuchia*, and the *Mesosuchia* the *Eusuchia*, in order of time.
>
> Now this is exactly what the geological evidence does prove . . .
>
> Thus the facts relating to the modifications which the Crocodilian type has undergone since its earliest known appearance, are exactly accordant with what is required by the theory of evolution; and the case of the Crocodiles is as cogent evidence of the actual occurrence of evolution as that of the Horses.

To understand Huxley's parasuchians, mesosuchians and eusuchians we need to revisit the classification debate. The taxonomy, or arrangement, of species arose from the need to identify formally the growing number of recognised species. In the preceding chapter we saw how the Linnaean classification system is still used today. The Linnaean system is a combination of two other classification systems, the phenetic and the cladistic. The phenetic system considers the physical structure of an animal or a plant. What does it look like? What is its behaviour in the wild? Many characteristics are considered, all equally important. On a phenetic level, crocodiles and lizards are very much alike, and not at all similar to birds.

The cladistic system is based on how long ago two organisms shared a common ancestor, and uses this to establish how closely related they are. On a cladistic level, then, crocodiles are closely related to birds and only very, very distantly to lizards. The evolutionary paths of crocodiles and birds parted in the Early Triassic, but both parted common ancestry with lizards somewhere in the Permian Era, some millions of years earlier.

The Linnaean system is the most subjective of the classification systems, but perhaps the most practical. As most classification is done using museum specimens, it is not possible to use a system which relies on observation of behaviour in the wild. Similarly, most fossils do not contain genetic material. Under the Linnaean system, crocodiles are classified as reptiles, along with lizards. This grouping helps researchers in the field investigating the animals' behaviour and biology but its subjective nature means that taxonomical debates continue to rage.

On a purely visual level, crocodilians *look* more like lizards than birds. However, as we saw in Chapter 3, unlike other reptiles crocodilians have a four-chambered heart, as do birds. Crocodilians also have an air sac system in their skulls, an elongated outer-ear canal and a muscular gizzard, as do their feathered relatives. Behaviourally, crocodilians and birds both build nests out of plant material and show some degree of care for their young. Together, crocodiles and birds are the last living descendants of the archosaurs.

The earliest signs of life are thought to have originated about 3.5 billion years ago. Fossils seem to have become prolific a little less than 600 million years ago. The first reptiles appear in the fossil record about 300 million years ago. As we saw earlier in the chapter, the first crocodilian, *Protosuchus*, appeared about 220 million years ago, with the ancestors of the modern crocodilians appearing about 80 million years ago, and *Crocodylus*, *Osteolaemus* and *Tomistoma* appearing about 10 million years ago.

The Palaeozoic Era extends from the time of the first fossils (over 500 million years ago) until the Permian Period, when a massive extinction of living species, sometimes referred to as the 'Great Dying', occurred about 245 million years ago. The Great Dying was followed by the Mesozoic Era, or the 'Age of the Reptiles', the latter part of which is also known as the 'Age of the Dinosaurs'. The Mesozoic Era is divided into the Triassic, Jurassic and Cretaceous Periods, and also ended in a massive extinction, about 65 million years ago.

With the disappearance of the dinosaurs, the Cenozoic Era began. Mammals, birds, insects and flowering plants proliferated, but the crocodilians survived. The diagram on page 139 shows a simplified vertebrate family tree. (The dotted lines indicate pieces of palaeontological guesswork.)

Palaeontological guesswork is supported by the fossil fragments that are continually coming to light. Huxley's progression of parasuchians to mesosuchians and then eusuchians, a progression distinguished by, among other things, differences in the structure of fossil vertebrae and the bony palate of the jaw, has been supported by the ages of the rocks in which the fossils were found.

The Triassic Period was the era of archosaurs known as 'thecodonts', large, scaly animals that flourished in the warm, dry desert environments. The term 'thecodont' is being replaced by the more accurate but much more long-winded 'basal archosauromorph'. In the interests of brevity, I'll stick to thecodont. Thecodonts came in different shapes and sizes but show enough crocodilian characteristics to be identified as the common ancestor of both the crocodiles and the dinosaurs. The thecodonts were, however, completely land-based.

The thecodonts were carnivores, whose teeth were set into sockets and therefore less likely to fall out while they were feeding. Not all archosaurs were carnivores. Some, such as the aetosaurs, were heavily armoured plant-eaters, ancestors of the dinosaurs familiar to us as *Stegosaurus* and *Ankylosaurus*. The modern crocodiles, too, are heavily armoured and scaly,

Geological time scale showing the evolution of the crocodilian

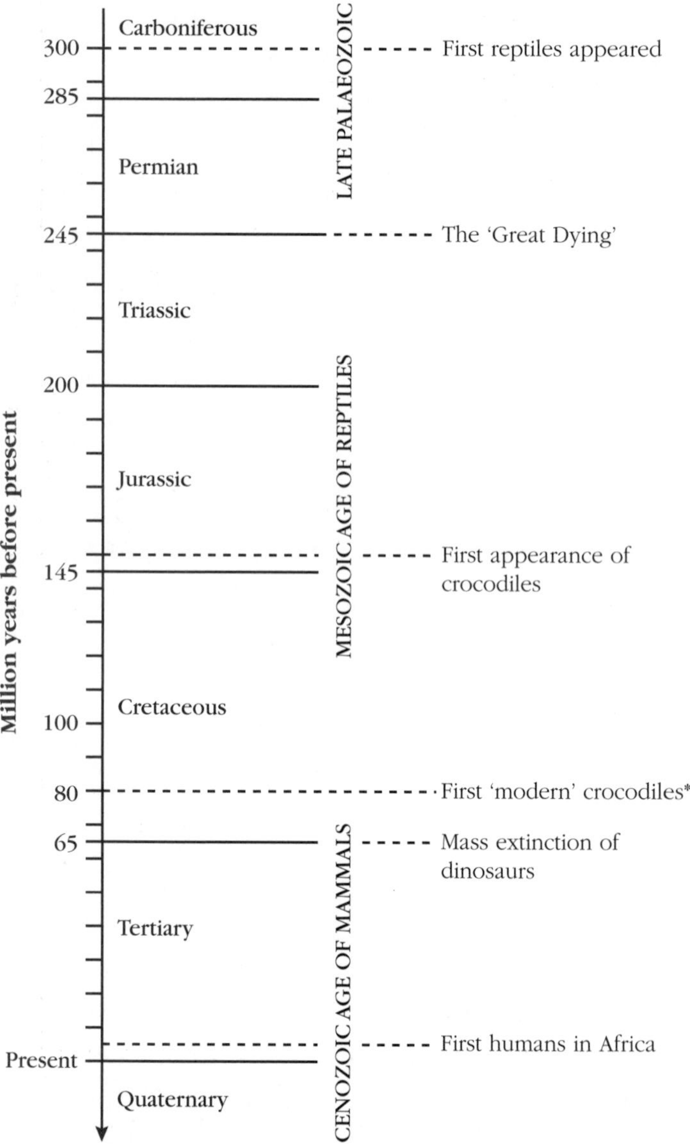

*The accepted date prior to the recent discovery of Steve Salisbury's Isisford crocodilian, said to date back nearly 100 million years before present.

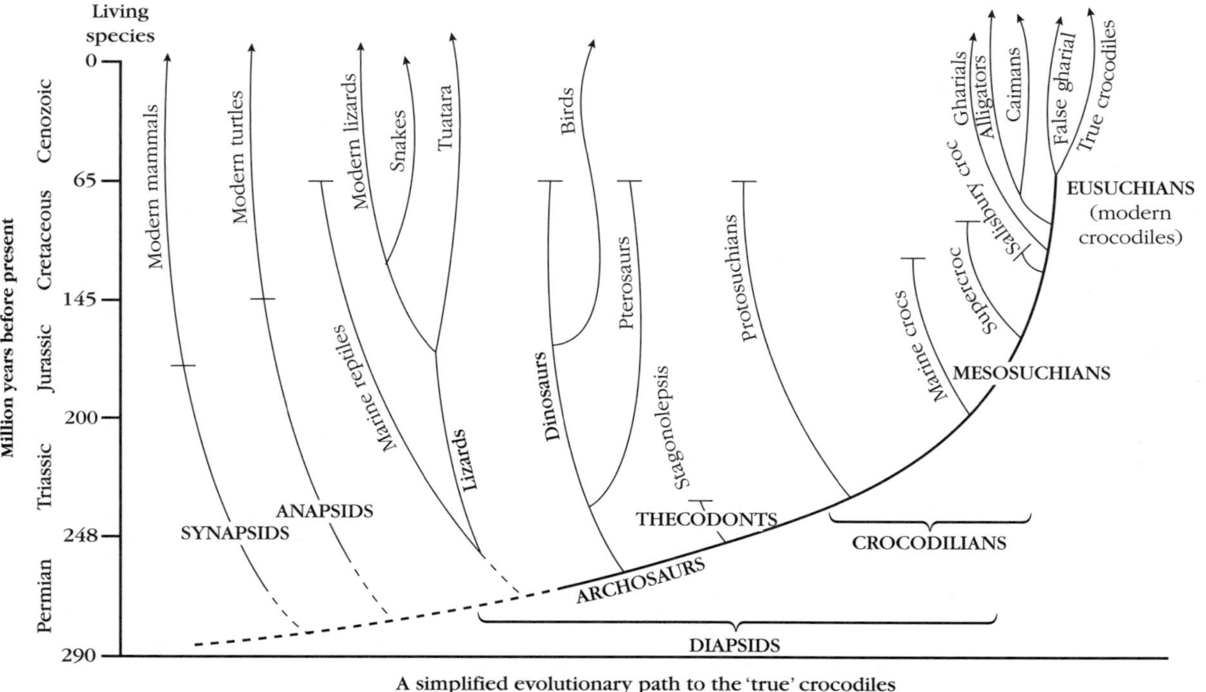

A simplified evolutionary path to the 'true' crocodiles

with a layer of bone mineralisation beneath the ridges or scutes running along their backs.

By the end of the Triassic Period the archosaurs had evolved into the dinosaurs and the protoavian pterosaurs. Many of the smaller branches of the crocodilian family tree, such as Huxley's *Stagonolepis*, disappeared into extinction. The Jurassic crocodilians included the first branch of the family to take to the water, the thalattosuchians. Many of the Jurassic crocodilians were enormous animals but, by the end of the Cretaceous Period, all had disappeared.

The Cretaceous Period was, truly, the era of the mesosuchians whose fossils have been found in large numbers in Europe, Africa and North America. The Middle Cretaceous saw the rise of a giant crocodilian, *Sarchosuchus imperator*, a creature now known affectionately as 'SuperCroc', while the Late Cretaceous Period saw the emergence of the eusuchians, such as *Deinosuchus*, and the split in the evolutionary tree that led to the modern families of crocodilians we know today.

There are still many dotted lines to be filled in on the evolutionary family tree, but with a fossil record dating back over 200 million years, the crocodilians have already played a vital role in our understanding of Darwin's revolutionary theory. Palaeontologists such as Steve Salisbury travel all over the world in search of the evidence that will allow them to block in these dotted lines.

One such travelling scientist is Paul Sereno. In 1997 he left the University of Chicago for the first of a series of expeditions into what is now the sub-Saharan desert in Niger, Africa. In the Middle Cretaceous Period, this arid zone would have teemed with life, swimming in lakes and rivers and foraging through semi-tropical wetlands. Sereno was on the trail of *Sarcosuchus imperator*, whose teeth and skull had been found thirty years earlier by a French team of palaeontologists. Sereno's team had barely begun to dig before they found fossils of SuperCroc jaws, each almost 2 metres long. They also found vertebrae, bones and individual scutes that were nearly 30 centimetres long, enough to build a picture of an animal that would have reached almost 12 metres in length and weighed over 17 000 kilograms. SuperCroc was so huge that it would have spent most of its time in the water, feeding on the other inhabitants of its lake or lying in wait for unwary small dinosaurs drinking at the water's edge.

SuperCroc has much to tell us about the ancient crocodilians, not least because of the diversity of crocodilian specimens found alongside him. Sereno's team found fossils from at least four crocodilian species, including an 8-centimetre long skull of a new species of dwarf crocodile. Although some crocodilians' territories can overlap, nowhere in the world do we find the same profusion of modern crocodilians in one place. There are still many pieces of the puzzle to put into place, which is why Sereno and other palaeontologists continue to hunt for the fossilised remains of extinct crocodilians. Unfortunately, indiscriminate hunting of some of our modern crocodilians means that more and more species are in danger of becoming extinct. Who are the crocodile hunters?

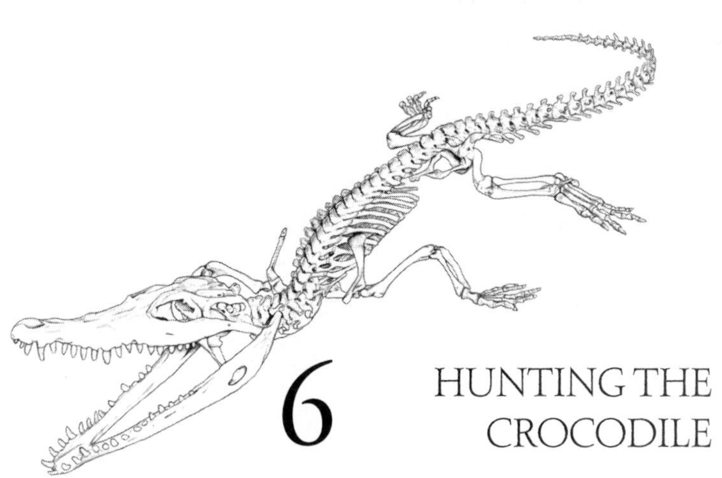

6 HUNTING THE CROCODILE

There are many and various ways of crocodile hunting; I will write only of that one way which I think most worthy of mention: the hunter baits a hook with a chine of pork, and lets it float into the midst of the river; he himself stays on the bank with a young live pig, which he beats. Hearing the cries of the pig, the crocodile goes after the sound and meets the chine, which it swallows; then the hunters pull the line. When the crocodile is drawn ashore, first of all the hunter smears its eyes over with mud; when this is done the quarry is very easily mastered, which, without that, is no light matter.

I do not know whether Tom Cole read Herodotus, or if he had, what he would have thought of the Egyptian hunting methods Herodotus describes here. Tom Cole was a crocodile hunter who used harpoons and guns to kill crocodiles in outback Australia. He left his native England for Australia in 1923 when he was only seventeen. He was not close to his father. In fact, it was two weeks after his departure before his father noticed his absence and asked about his whereabouts. His mother replied that he had gone to Australia. His father never mentioned his name again. So Cole tells us in his autobiography *Hell West and Crooked*, where he recounts his experiences as a drover, station hand and hunter of buffalo and crocodiles.

The crocodile skin industry was in its infancy in Australia, and the crocodiles were still plentiful. Cole was working on an outback station in northern Queensland hunting buffalo when he received a letter from a Mr Grant, offering to buy crocodile skins.

> He said his company would pay one shilling and sixpence an inch, measurement taken across the belly. A diagram was enclosed showing the skinning method and a few details on curing.
>
> Gaden and Jennings were the first to take it on commercially and I had heard them talking about it. There were plenty to be had; riding past a waterhole where buffalo carcasses were lying from previous shooting it was a common sight to see crocodiles tearing at them. On our approach they would scuttle away quickly into the water.

It is often mistakenly assumed that crocodiles don't have tongues. However, in this picture of a saltwater crocodile's gape the tongue, attached to the lower jaw, is clearly visible. (Courtesy Adam Britton)

The powerful jaws of the Australian saltwater crocodile can easily crush through the shells of crabs and turtles. (Courtesy Adam Britton)

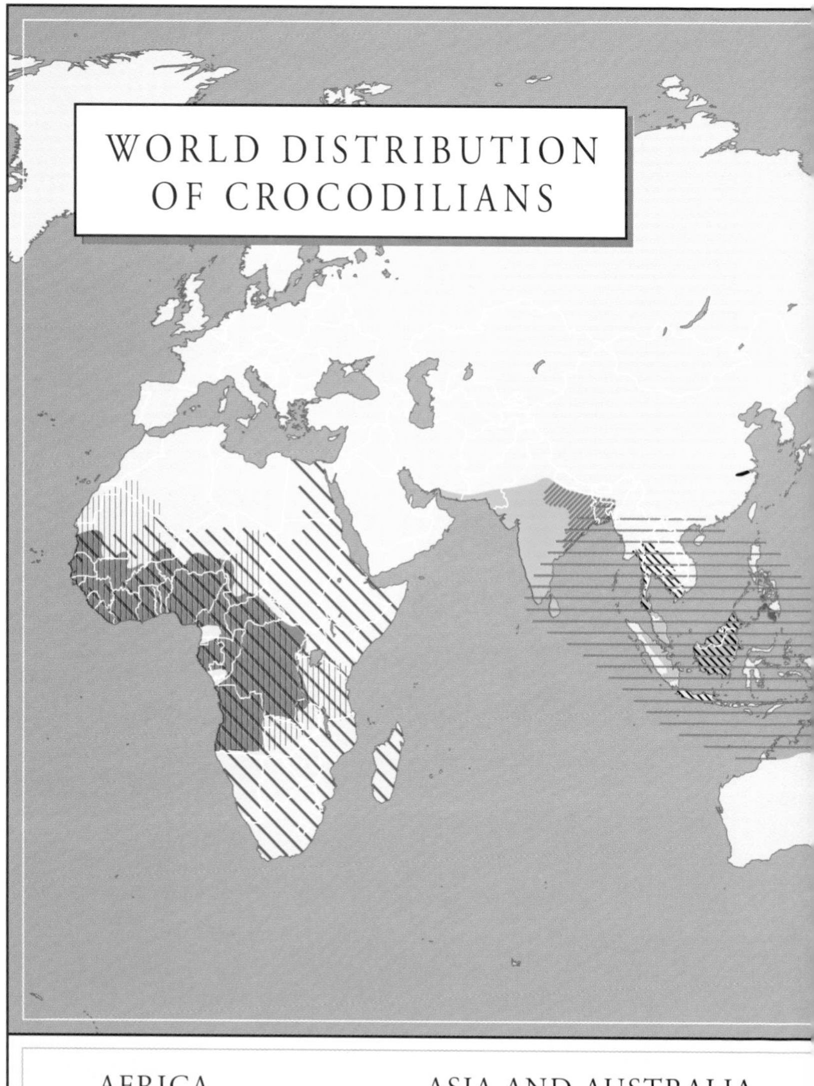

AFRICA

African slender -snouted crocodile

Nile crocodile

Dwarf crocodile

ASIA AND AUSTRALIA

Chinese alligator

Johnston's crocodile

Philippine crocodile

New Guinea crocodile

Mugger crocodile

Estuarine croc

Siamese croco

False gharial

Gharial

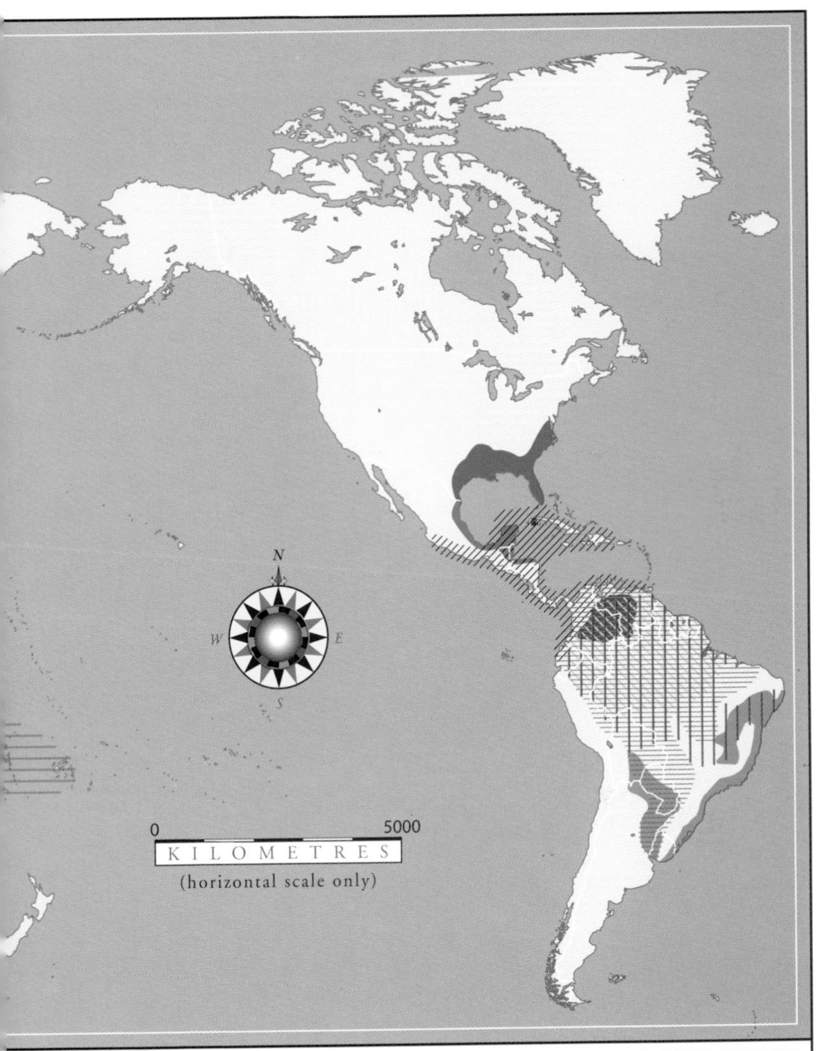

NORTH AND SOUTH AMERICA

- American alligator
- Common caiman
- Broad-snouted caiman
- Black caiman
- Cuvier's dwarf caiman
- Shneider's dwarf caiman
- American crocodile
- Orinoco crocodile
- Morelet's crocodile
- Cuban crocodile

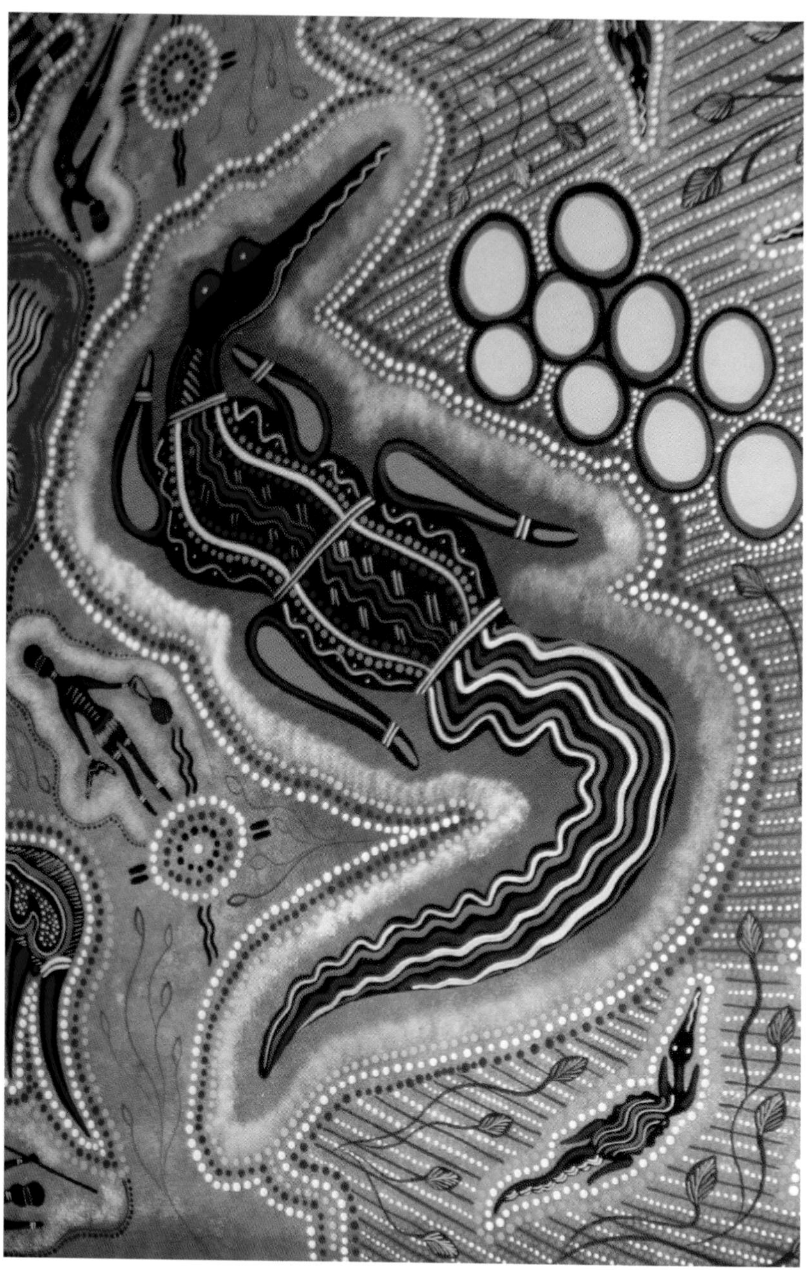

Where the land meets the sea, *by contemporary Australian Aboriginal artist C.J. Archer, depicts Aboriginals hunting a crocodile for food, in its natural habitat, between the land and the sea. Note the crocodile eggs and hatchlings to the right of the crocodile. (Courtesy Jenny Mairs)*

This detail from a reproduction of The Papyrus of Hunefer *(c. 1370 BC) from the Ancient Egyptian 'Book of the Dead' depicts the Hall of Ma'at where the judgement of the dead was performed. Here we see Anubis leading Hunefer to the scales of Ma'at where his heart will be weighed against the feather of truth. If his heart is found unworthy it will be devoured by Ammut, the demon with the head of a crocodile, crouching nearby in wait.*

The Chinese alligator is an increasingly rare, isolated population found on the banks of the Yangtze River, with perhaps no more than a few hundred individuals remaining in the wild. (Courtesy Adam Britton)

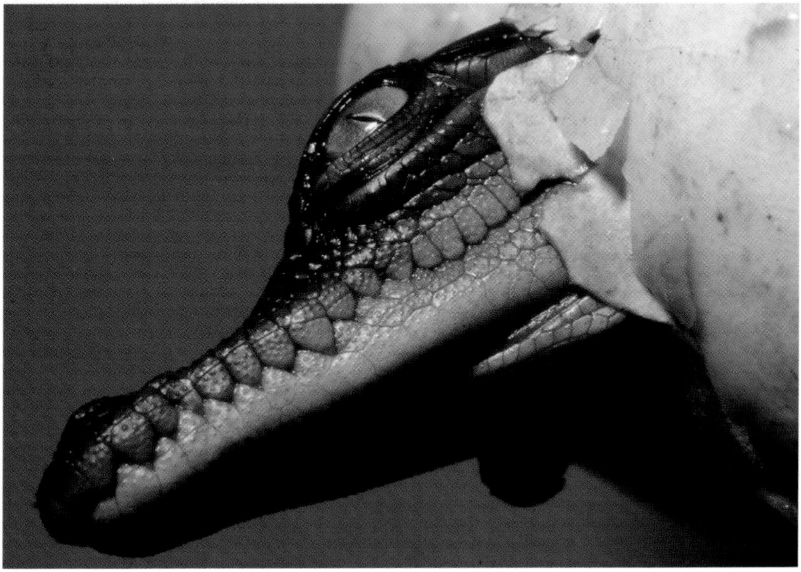

A young crocodile hatchling emerges from its egg, following an incubation period of between seventy and ninety-five days. (Courtesy Adam Britton)

A mother carries her freshly hatched baby in her jaws to the river for its first swim. (Courtesy Adam Britton)

A saltwater crocodile snatches an unfortunate bat from a branch overhanging the lagoon, much like the attack described by Benjamin Helpman in Chapter 1, almost two centuries earlier. (Courtesy Adam Britton)

> At that time nothing was known about spotlight shooting at night, which in later years decimated them until protective measures were brought in. Gaden and Jennings' boys got them by spearing, though I had never seen them doing it.

Cole assigned some of his team to start hunting crocodiles while the others finished their buffalo contract. Cole had great respect for the Aboriginal members of his team and their bush skills. Having made harpoons and a raft fashioned from paperbark lashed together with vines, the team was ready to tackle the large, saltwater crocodiles which inhabit the freshwater rivers right down to the salt water of the sea. Cole describes how Bamboo Charlie, the senior Aborigine on the team, led their first crocodile hunt.

> It was explained to me by Charlie that we would start at the first crack of dawn—piccaninny daylight. It was essential there was not the slightest breeze to ruffle the surface of the water and the excitement was such on the first morning of our operations that everybody was sitting around the campfire waiting anxiously for dawn to break.
>
> As soon as there was enough light to see, Bamboo Charlie stepped onto his strange craft and poled his way out to the middle. He reversed the harpoon shaft and started thrashing the surface of the water furiously. Very soon a line of bubbles appeared on the surface—something was moving along the muddy bottom. That something was a crocodile! Then

the bubbles stopped. Charlie quickly reversed his harpoon and held it poised over the water as the flimsy craft glided over the bubbles. When he got to the spot where the bubbles stopped, he drove the harpoon down in the water with all his strength.

Charlie's thrust was accurate and there was a mighty swirl as the rope snaked out, more than half of it disappearing into the water. He poled his way to the bank and gave the rope to one of the boys waiting excitedly. Willing hands came to his assistance and it became a one-sided tug-of-war.

With a lot of shrieking from men, women and children, a ten-foot crocodile was dragged to the bank thrashing wildly. I quickly dispatched it with a bullet to the head.

The harpoon, which was firmly embedded in its back, was cut out and Charlie, with a great smile of satisfaction, poled out into the middle of the billabong again. Quickly he had harpooned another one, a bit smaller than the first but nevertheless a useful size.

By about 10 am a breeze sprang up and ruffled the surface of the water to such an extent that the telltale bubbles could not be seen, so we stopped hunting. We had five and they were all skinned, salted down and stacked away in the shade.

I had to get back to finishing Freer's contract and left Singing Man Billy with the crocodile hunters. They got eleven more over the next two days and Charlie said the hole was cleaned out, so I moved them over to another good lagoon a few miles away.

Cole and his team continued to clean the crocodiles out of waterholes and lagoons without any concern for leaving some to breed. It was this gung-ho approach that sounded the death knell for entire populations of crocodilians all over the world. Conservation came slowly.

Crocodile hunting did not start with the white man and his gun. Indigenous peoples around the world have hunted both the saltwater and freshwater crocodilians for thousands of years as part of their diet. They did not, however, engage in wholesale slaughter of the animals for their skins.

To write their book *Australian Crocodiles: A natural history*, Dr Grahame Webb and his co-author, Charlie Manolis, drew on thirty years of research on crocodiles. They talk with respect about the understanding of the indigenous people for these creatures. Recognised and respected for their close relationship with the land and water, Australian Aboriginal tribes know every nest site of the crocodiles in their area. They will collect eggs and kill the female for food, claiming that the nest site will be taken up by a younger female. Research on the freshwater crocodile has added support to this claim indicating a ready supply in many populations of sub-adult females in wait for a nest site.

Crocodiles appear to respond to the threat of a hunter in their territory. Webb and Manolis note: 'Aboriginal hunting may well be responsible for striking variation in the inherent level of wariness seen in crocodiles from the time they hatch. Freshwater Crocodiles from areas that were heavily occupied by Aborigines are a good deal more wary than those from areas that were not heavily occupied.'

While I was researching this book, many of the people I spoke to who deal with crocodilians on a daily basis talked about their high level of awareness. Whether it is inherent or acquired behaviour, or maybe a bit of both, they are certainly very cautious when danger is indicated. Hunters tell of the way the crocodiles and alligators become far harder to find, the threatened animal hiding in vegetation or mud, or moving to safer waters. It must be remembered that these are highly territorial creatures. Forcing them into the territories of other crocodiles to escape the hunters will embroil them in battles with their own kind. With a suddenly overcrowded territory and no escape route, deaths are inevitable.

Those who have to travel overland to find new territories face other dangers. Tom Cole recounts an episode from his very early days of hunting crocodiles. He had been chasing buffalo when his horse, Gambler, shied and swerved sharply. He looked for what could have startled the horse so severely.

Cole was astonished to see a fairly large crocodile dead in the grass. Only metres further on he found another. Then another and another. Eleven dead crocodiles were discovered in a very short distance. Cole notes that crocodiles become wary of hunters. They will move from their waterholes when they feel threatened, the survivors from one waterhole fleeing to the next, invading the territories of other crocodiles. The disturbance of new, stressed animals may have raised the fears of those in the waterhole the hunters had not yet reached. They headed for safer waters or stayed well out of sight, making hunting more difficult.

When Cole was hunting in a lagoon at Banyon Point, the distance to watering places which had not been hunted was just too far. At least eleven didn't make it. They left at night, but were not safe by day. As the sun's heat became intense, the dehydration would have killed them.

Like the indigenous Australians, native peoples all over the world have hunted crocodiles and their relatives as a normal part of the daily lives. Hunting serves a variety of purposes: it provides meat for food, fat for fuel, skins for clothing, and protection from an aggressive man-eater. More recently the skins have provided a source of income when sold for leather. As we saw in Chapter 2, this close contact with the crocodilians is reflected in the culture of the local people. This is true even of those who share the crocodilians' habitats but do not eat them, as they are almost always dependent on the water from the rivers for drinking, washing and watering their crops.

Crocodiles are feared and respected adversaries. In recognition of the risks involved in a crocodile hunt, many tribes donned spiritual armour and protected themselves with elaborate rituals. In Borneo the safety of those living by rivers demanded that man-eating crocodiles be hunted and killed. The responsibility for hunting down a killer rested with the witchdoctor. After he had prepared himself spiritually, the witchdoctor would start hunting crocodiles. He used a lance to spear any animal he caught on a baited hook and then examined his kill's stomach contents. When he found evidence of human remains, the remaining crocodiles were offered a cat to show they were not being hunted anymore and peace between the villagers and the crocodiles returned—until the next local was killed.

Pakistani hunters of the Sind tribe, hunting the less aggressive mugger and gharial, would float their crafts over their prey and force it to burrow into the mud. On their small floating vessels, with nets and poles ready, the hunters would surround the animal, now buried in the mud of the river floor. There it could then be trapped with bamboo stakes, ready for divers to loop rope around its body while under water. The animal was then dragged from the water and killed on land with long-handled axes. In Sri Lanka, some of the more daring hunters crawled into a mugger's burrow, tied ropes around the hiding mugger and dragged it out.

For centuries hunters have known that they would only be able to overcome the great crocodilians by stealth or subterfuge. The back of the mouth and the vulnerable underbelly are the only parts of the crocodilian unprotected by its armour of bony scutes and scales. A crocodilian that can be baited or lured into a trap can then be overcome by lances or spears, or sheer weight of numbers. All forms of nets and traps are used to snare the crocodilians for the kill. Large crocodilians which are caught in a net or trap will struggle violently, often exhausting themselves. They can get into such oxygen debt that they die. Crocodilians can drown, and are often found dead when they have been unable to surface quickly. This may be the result of deliberate trapping or, as is often reported in the case of the Indian mugger, the animal may get tangled in fishing nets while attempting to feed on the catch. In India hunters trapped the gharial by submerging nets in the water at the river's edge, where the animals are known to come ashore to bask. Fishermen on the Ghagra River have been reported as burying hooks attached to long ropes in the sand at the basking sites. When the gharials were basking, the fishermen would pull on the long ropes. The hooks would snag in the gharials' bellies, enabling an easy kill.

Seminole Indians in North America created funnel-shaped waterways with branches, forcing the American alligators into an S-shaped bend where meat or fish had been placed as bait. Unable to turn or back out, the alligator could then be speared. The Roman historian Pliny records pygmies, who hunted Africa's Nile crocodile, as using wooden spears to dispatch their cornered prey. As the crocodile bellowed in rage and fear the hunter would thrust his spear into the back of the beast's mouth. This method is still in use today by those who do not have access to high-powered rifles. As we saw in John Lort Stokes's description of his 'alligator' kill, ordinary percussion rifles have little impact against crocodilian armour.

Over the past 150 years, the hunting of crocodiles has decimated local populations. The Philippine crocodile faces extinction in the wild, while the Siamese crocodile was virtually wiped out by hunters by the middle of last century. In Australia crocodile hunting as a sport became popular in the nineteenth century but as sporting hunters were few and far between and the crocodiles plentiful, this did not have the huge impact seen later with wholesale commercial hunting. Naturalists writing about India from early last century tell of the art of hunting crocodiles of all species: muggers, gharials and saltwater crocodiles. However, the demise of the saltwater crocodile populations in India is due more to loss of habitat than uncontrolled hunting, which was never a huge commercial practice.

As leather processing techniques improved, hunting crocodilians became a profitable venture. Crocodile leather shoes, belts and handbags became very fashionable. In most cases, the skin of the animal's underbelly is used as the upper body hide is rendered almost useless by its bony ridges or scutes.

The numbers of crocodiles killed for their skin are staggering. As we saw in Tom Cole's reminiscences of hunting Australian saltwater crocodiles at the turn of the twentieth century, the hunters, through their wholesale slaughter of the salties, almost destroyed their own industry. Species extinction is still a real threat to crocodilians today in areas where commercial hunting is uncontrolled and regulations, should they exist, are not enforced.

The American alligator has been hunted for centuries for both its skin and its meat. The Native Americans ate the meat

The belly of a young saltwater crocodile, showing the skin which will become high-quality leather. (Courtesy Damian Kelly)

as a normal part of their diet. With a similar texture to chicken, but a fishier taste, (as we shall see in Chapter 8), the alligator is not the only crocodilian now farmed for this purpose.

The skin of the American alligator is particularly good for tanning into leather for handbags, boots, belts and other items. State trade records for Florida and Louisiana, the home of the alligators, show skins being sold in the Miami area for seven American dollars each as early as 1800. The profitability of the trade meant that the American alligators were slaughtered in their tens of thousands every year. In a fifty-year span, from 1880, well over three million alligators were killed in Louisiana, while Florida wasn't far behind.

It wasn't foresight or a desire to conserve indigenous species which reined in the threat hunting posed to the survival of the species, but simple economics. As the numbers of alligators fell and skins became in short supply, prices soared. The fashion industry's demand for alligator skins at the end of the nineteenth century was such that enterprising hunters travelled far and wide to meet the demand. The skins of the American crocodile and Central and South American species, such as Morelet's crocodile, were brazenly labelled 'alligator skin'.

Culling at such a level could not be sustained, and had the hunting not been regulated it is unlikely there would be any American alligators today.

In 1944 alligator hunting was banned in America during the breeding season. Although a number of populations had regained some ground, in 1961 Florida introduced legislation making alligator hunting illegal. Poaching became rife until federal legislation to stop skins crossing state borders was enacted in 1969. By 1973 crocodiles and alligators in America were protected under the federal Endangered Species Act. Florida now has strict laws controlling the harvesting of alligators. The animals are farmed for their meat and skins, and some hunting is permitted in very limited and well-controlled hunts, with all hunters requiring permits. Louisiana's hunters are all licensed, and the legal alligator skins tagged, to keep the populations at a sustainable level.

Moving through Mexico and into Central America, the American crocodile and Morelet's crocodile were also targeted for their valuable skins, although habitat destruction also took its toll. With variable success, management programs and protection schemes are arresting the decline in numbers, although the illegal trade continues, with grisly 'curios' such as key rings made from hatchlings' heads proving popular in Europe. In the past, South America's caiman populations have also been affected by hunting, with the black caiman hunted almost to extinction for its skin. Although now a protected species, the skins are still readily available in markets in French Guiana, without the head. Hence it is impossible to tell at a glance whether the skin is that of the protected black caiman or the legally marketed common caiman, which has a different skull shape.

The common caiman's actually benefited due to the commercial over-hunting of the other species in the middle of last century. The bony scutes on the belly of the common caiman limited the value of its skin for leather, hence they did not suffer from the uncontrolled hunting which decimated other, more desirable, species. However, now that these other species are, in the main, protected, the common caiman is harvested in huge numbers, supplying most of the hides for America. Ironically the leather of the common caiman is now one of those often labelled 'American alligator'.

One of the largest of the crocodiles, the Orinoco crocodile of Colombia and Venezuela, was hunted ruthlessly for its skin. The hunters dragged the animals from their burrows during the dry season, their breeding season. Over-exploitation in the middle of the twentieth century has meant that the species is now severely 'at risk'. The Orinoco crocodile's range is so limited that, even with protection, population recovery has been very slow and may not be sustainable.

Hunters headed even further afield as skins became scarcer. After the Second World War, they began to target the widespread African Nile crocodile. It is estimated that up to three million may have been killed by professional hunters for their skins. Some countries encouraged the hunters, their governments hoping to wipe out an animal considered a 'pest'. As early as 1900 the Natal Government offered a bounty scheme under which hunters were rewarded not only for each dead crocodile but also for any eggs they collected. Many of the crocodiles fell victim to baits laced with strychnine. Natal has now set up the Ndumu Game Reserve, which runs research and restocking programs. In Angola, however, the once healthy Nile crocodile populations of the Cuanza River have been wiped out.

Around the middle of the twentieth century, Belgian-ruled Congo emerged as the world's major supplier of crocodile skins, supplied from their Nile crocodile population. With close to 80 per cent of the global market coming from the central African country, hunters came in their hundreds. However, from 1960, the escalating political unrest after independence made the country unsafe for foreigners. Alligators were being protected in America, so interest turned to a country with large crocodile populations, no regulations and a stable political climate—Australia.

Australian hunters had already made some forays into the

world market for crocodile skins, and had discovered that saltwater crocodile skins were particularly valuable. Almost all other species of crocodilian have osteoderms in the belly scales, but the saltwater crocodile never does, making its skin reliably good for leather production.

Crocodile skins are measured across the belly and priced according to width. Within the five years following 1959, a saltwater crocodile skin more than tripled in value.

As the populations of saltwater crocodiles were being depleted, the Australian freshwater crocodiles were basking in the sun, protected by a skin which was too brittle for contemporary tanning processes. Unfortunately for the freshwater crocodile, tanning processes improved. A single waterhole could contain a hundred crocodiles, and the hunters would take every one for tanning. The freshwater crocodiles soon became endangered in many areas. As the waterholes were emptied, hunters ventured further inland. The once plentiful populations were over-exploited and numbers fell drastically.

Australian hunters targeted the Papua New Guinea populations of the saltwater crocodile from the mid 1950s, effectively establishing the crocodile skin industry in this country. With declining numbers in the large waterways accessible to motor boats, the PNG locals ventured into the more remote areas to hunt the salties. When the saltwater crocodiles became scarce, the hunters turned their attention to the less valuable New Guinea crocodile, depleting its populations until legislation was introduced in the 1970s to protect it.

The New Guinea crocodile is now being farmed. It is hoped that this industry will help the native people, who lost not only their income from the trade in crocodile skins as the crocodile populations disappeared, but also a traditional food source. Both species are now recovering in Papua New Guinea.

The Western Australian Government passed legislation to protect freshwater crocodiles in 1962, followed by the Northern Territory in 1963. The saltwater crocodiles were protected in Western Australia in 1969 and the Northern Territory in 1971. Queensland is the only other state in which crocodiles are found. It was not until 1974 that the Queensland Government finally recognised the threat uncontrolled hunting posed to its crocodiles and legislated to protect the remaining populations of both species. For the preceding twelve years, however, an illegal trade in skins from theoretically protected states had been marketed through Queensland. With regulations in place in all crocodile-inhabited states, the trade was finally controlled. It must be acknowledged, though, that the crocodiles had become so rare that the hunters were finding it hard to make a living.

Despite the fact that the Australian saltwater and freshwater crocodiles were over-hunted to dangerous levels, they are more fortunate that many of their crocodilian relatives. As their outback habitat remains almost untouched, the populations have been able to become re-established to the extent that neither species is now considered endangered. So, with the populations secure, a new debate arises. Should limited, controlled hunting be permitted?

Dr Grahame Webb runs the Crocodylus Tourist Park on the outskirts of Darwin and has been working with crocodiles for over thirty years. He supports the Northern Territory Government's request to the federal government that it be allowed to offer a small number of hunting permits for safari-type experiences to well-paying foreign hunters. He says that 'armchair conservationists' in urban areas do not understand. 'It's feel good stuff that has no relationship to the situation here. I don't know why we make fools of ourselves by persisting with this extreme green view about killing any animal.'

Territory landowners are granted permits to kill hundreds of crocodiles every year, yet at the time of writing, the federal government was still refusing the twenty-five permits requested for special hunting safaris. Webb finds this incredible. 'A landowner can pull the trigger and kill a croc that is chasing his staff around and eating his stock but a safari hunter, willing to pay thousands of dollars, cannot.'

International wildlife trade is a multi-million dollar industry. Most of the world's countries have now recognised that uncontrolled exploitation of wildlife will mean that many species will not see out this century. Many have already gone forever, or are so depleted in numbers that their extinction in the wild is now certain. An international agreement, CITES (the Convention on International Trade in Endangered Species of Wild Fauna and Flora), aimed at controlling the trade which contributes to this tragedy has been formalised. It covers not only trade in animals and plants, but also the products made from them. From wooden musical instruments to crocodile handbags, it is almost impossible for the consumer to know if their purchase is from a farm or from the wild, and whether it has any impact on the existing population. Unfortunately many don't care. How many of those who would choose to buy a stuffed crocodile lamp stand would bother to ask if this was once the juvenile of a protected species?

By February 2006, according to the CITES website, www.cites.org, 169 countries had joined CITES and voluntarily undertaken to adhere to its rules. It is hoped that even species that are not currently officially listed as endangered will be protected by the spirit of cooperation which is the basis of the CITES philosophy. Trade between countries of CITES-listed species requires permits and tight controls, which have already been shown to improve the status of these endangered species.

The CITES regulations accord varying degrees of protection to over 30 000 species, which are divided into three levels of protection known as Appendices. All twenty-three crocodilian species are protected in the top two Appendices. CITES Appendix I lists those species that are threatened with extinction and it is only in exceptional circumstances that any trade in these species would be permitted. Appendix II lists species that are not necessarily threatened with extinction, but in which trade must be controlled so that their populations are not exploited beyond the level at which the species could survive.

Seventeen crocodilians are included in Appendix I, although there are a few species for which some countries have a CITES Appendix II level of protection. The saltwater crocodile is one of those. Although still endangerd in countries such as Irian Jaya and Sri Lanka, the saltwater crocodile is no longer considered to be under threat of extinction in Australia, Indonesia or Papua New Guinea, and hence has Appendix II classification for these countries. The Appendix II listing is designed to ensure that this will not happen again. The CITES agreement includes a blanket statement that any crocodilian not listed in Appendix I is automatically included in Appendix II. The Australian freshwater crocodile, for example, is protected at that level.

The fact that agreements such as CITES can be formalised and adhered to on a voluntary basis shows that our attitude to hunting has changed greatly over the last century. Hunting for pleasure used to be considered masculine and brave, an attitude few would admit to having now. It was an attitude that reflected a belief not only in the superiority of man amongst his fellow men, but in the lowly status of the beasts of which he sought to rid the world.

Crocodiles were seen as 'fair game' for a number of reasons. Not only were they mighty and powerful creatures, but they inspired fear, awe and loathing in their human adversaries. In

My African Journey! Winston Churchill wrote of crocodiles: 'I avow, with what regrets may be necessary, an active hatred of these brutes and a desire to kill them.' The professional Scottish hunter J.B. Hunter wrote about the crocodiles in Africa: 'It is strange there should be a common enemy to both man and beast, but it is so, in that hideous monster, the crocodile. He can be aptly described as a loathsome beast, unloved and feared by all.'

A crocodile attack is a fearsome thing to witness—we have all seen images on nature programs of the silent predator lunging from the water, its hapless prey being dragged into the depths in a swirl of hooves, spray and teeth. Man has, traditionally, been the supreme predator. The fact that there is an animal who can take a man as easily as a zebra calf or an antelope would inspire some of the fear and loathing voiced by those who hunted them.

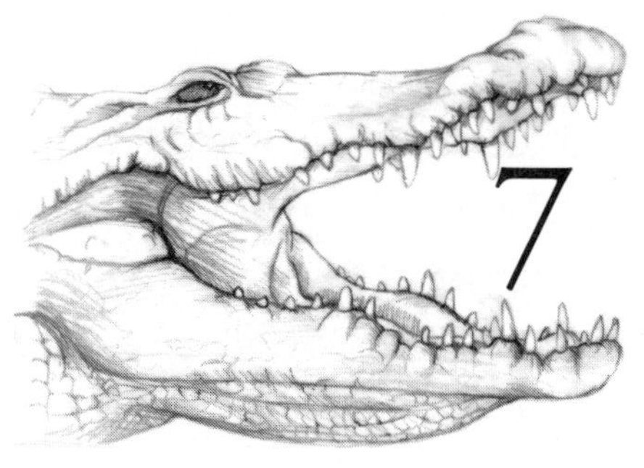

7 CROCODILE ATTACKS

A group of people came to the mouth of the King River where they needed to ferry themselves across. They had only one canoe. One man was repeatedly refused permission to go on the canoe. He became angry and in his rage decided to become a crocodile. Having swum up the river, he made a fire and heated ironwood roots. He pounded them and placed them on his nose to craft it into the crocodile's powerful jaws. Diving into the river, he became a real crocodile, or gunbiribiri. *Returning to the mouth of the river, he capsized the canoe of those who had so wronged him. Eating those who fell into the river, he exacted his revenge. With a threat to kill any others he could catch, the crocodile established himself as a creature to fear.*

North of Arnhem Land in the Auray Bay is Goulburn Island, Australia, where the people tell this legend of the formation of the saltwater crocodile.

There are many stories that promote the idea that crocodilians are creatures to be feared, some more factual than others. It was in Burma, early in 1945, that one of the more gruesome stories of the Second World War emerged. The Japanese were in retreat. A thousand soldiers were driven into a mangrove swamp between Burma and Ramree Island, blocked in by a British Royal Navy brigade. The Japanese were in search of their rescue ships when they met an enemy they had not encountered before: the saltwater crocodile.

Night fell and the crocodiles came in their hundreds, slaughtering the Japanese intruders. All night long the attack continued, and by morning only about twenty of the thousand soldiers remained alive. Some drowned, some may have been shot, but the vast majority fell victim to the deadly crocodiles. It was a massacre of the most bloodiest order.

Or so the story is oft told. Research into this story will soon lead to the conclusion that there is little truth in the tale. There were retreating Japanese and they did pass through swampland on Ramree Island. There was great loss of life, but the details are scant and the degree of guilt of the crocodiles is far from verified.

Whenever you have large man-killing beasts to fuel the imagination, as crocodiles and alligators are wont to do, you will get a range of wildly fanciful stories about ferocious attacks. Yet they do attack and they do kill. So where does the truth lie in the stories and where does the fancy begin? And what is a crocodile attack really like?

Although the American alligator, the black caiman, the mugger, the Orinoco crocodile and the American crocodile have reportedly killed humans on rare occasions, the occurrences of such attacks are few and far between. The most dangerous of the crocodilian species are, by a long way, the saltwater and the Nile crocodiles. In fact the Nile crocodile kills more humans than all other crocodilian species combined, but still only in the order of a few hundred per year. Given that the animal is widespread across a vast continent whose people depend on the rivers for water, food and transport, these tragic events are almost inevitable. Interestly, the hippopotamus kills more people in Africa than the crocodile. In a battle between the two deadly creatures, the hippopotamus will usually emerge the victor.

While crocodiles do attack humans, they may not have initially been aggressive towards them. Many researchers, hunters and wildlife managers comment that crocodiles are much harder to see in places where they are not used to the presence of humans. When the unfamiliar human species appears, the crocodilians are usually quick to disappear. However, where we have started to take over their territories, the crocodilians have become more used to having humans around. They have become less afraid and the number of attacks has increased. A crouching human comes to resemble their more familiar prey.

The saltwater crocodile is not as aggressive as the Nile crocodile, but fatal attacks have been recorded across the full extent of its range, from Asia to Australia. In Australia there is rarely more than a single fatality in a year and some years pass with none. A fatal attack arouses a mixed reaction. Some claim the animal is only acting on instinct and should be left alone—we should avoid them totally. Others claim the animal will keep killing now it has the taste—we should kill it first. Yet others claim no-one can be safe where there are crocodiles—we should kill them all!

Crocodile attacks were an accepted part of the northern Australian river environment. In Chapter 6 we met Tom Cole whose aboriginal assistant, Bamboo Charlie, helped him shoot buffalos and crocodiles while also working as a station hand. Bamboo Charlie had years of bush experience and an understanding of crocodiles. Despite this, Charlie's wife, Maudie, fell victim to a large saltwater crocodile. Cole remembers being notified of the tragedy:

> I was busy drafting horses when several boys came running breathlessly up to the yard calling, 'Boss! Boss! Maudie go finish, big fella alligator eat him finish!'
>
> The shock of this only took a second or so to sink in. I was horrified. It only seemed like a few moments ago when

they had set off for the river laughing, joking, scolding their dogs, calling to the children to hurry.

Maudie taken by a crocodile—I just couldn't believe it. I quickly saddled a horse and rode across to the river; the plain was partly flooded and I had to leave my horse and walk the last few hundred yards.

I reached the mangroves where they were all grouped together crying and wailing. I picked out a fellow who seemed fairly well in control of himself and asked what had happened.

He said they had started to swim and were fairly well strung out. The children were clinging to logs that were being pushed by the men; the women were behind. Maudie and another, sharing a log, were the last of all. As far as I could understand Maudie and her companion were only about twenty yards from the bank. The crocodile came up behind and swam over the top of her, grasping her with its forefeet, and dived. She never uttered a sound, a moment later it reappeared briefly with Maudie in its jaws. They never saw her again.

They all came back from the river just before sundown. As I'd expected, they had not sighted the crocodile. In the morning Bamboo Charlie asked for a rifle; he wanted to stay on the river until he saw it and shoot it but I felt sure it wouldn't show up for a day or so. He agreed with me but I think he felt he had some kind of duty to keep watch.

I suggested he go out and shoot a wild pig, there were plenty about, to which he agreed. His shooting licence was still current—not that that would have bothered me. He came back with two, a young sow and an old boar.

They dressed the young pig and I took half. They had a wailing feast that night with half the young sow and half of the boar. What was left they put in a couple of bags and took it to the river where they hung the meat in the mangroves high enough above the ground to keep it from being taken. It putrefied quickly, in the hot sun and in a couple of days was an effective attraction. On the second day they shot a young crocodile about eight feet long, but didn't bother opening it up.

On the fourth day, just before sundown, the man-eater appeared. It only took one shot. They opened it up and inside found a quantity of Maudie's bones, which they washed carefully and wrapped in paperbark. Most of that night was spent crying and wailing and in the morning Bamboo Charlie said they were leaving. He asked if I would like to see the bones, but I couldn't bring myself to look at them. She was such a dear old thing.

They all left together. Their intention was to cross the river close to Jim Jim junction where it was shallow and easily crossed. They had been put off swimming for some time.

Few survive a crocodile attack, especially when tossed by a death roll. When a crocodile has a large, struggling prey in its jaws, it will thrust its own body into a rolling motion, sinking its teeth deeper into its catch. Throwing the prey off balance, the crocodile will drag it into the water, rolling and thrashing over and over until the prey stops struggling. If the victim does escape, it will certainly bear horrific injuries as a result of the roll.

In 1985 Val Plumwood was paddling a canoe in the East Alligator River, Kakadu National Park, Australia, looking at rock art. She is one of the very few who have survived to tell what it feels like to be tossed around in a death roll while in the jaws of a crocodile. Recounting the attack, she said:

> I was in a canoe on a side channel of the East Alligator River in Kakadu, looking for an Aboriginal rock art site. I had been out the previous day and it had been idyllic. This day began with drizzle, which progressed into torrential rain. By early afternoon I had a strong feeling of being watched and suddenly the canoe seemed flimsy. I had a sense of danger or vulnerability and decided I wanted to go back.
>
> I started paddling back down the channel and hadn't got far when I saw what looked like a stick ahead of me. As I was swept towards it I saw eyes and realised it was a crocodile.
>
> I was almost past it when there was this great blow on the side of the canoe. I paddled furiously but it followed, bashing on the canoe. I looked for a place to get out, but couldn't see one. I felt sheer terror. I saw a tree growing from the water near the bank and thought maybe I could leap into it. I got ready to jump and as I did so, the crocodile came up close. I looked straight into its eyes and it looked

straight into mine. It had beautiful golden-flecked eyes. I remember those vividly.

I did the thing you're advised to do, to try to look fearsome: I waved my arms and shouted. It might work with tigers but it doesn't work with crocodiles.

Then I jumped, but it got me in mid-jump. I saw this blur, a flash of teeth and water as it grabbed me between the legs and took me down for a death roll. I thought: 'I'm not food, I'm a human being; I don't believe this.'

There was searing pain, but the worst thing was the roll, which seemed to last forever. It pushes water in your lungs and it felt like my arms and legs were coming off. When it finished, my head came clear of the water and I coughed the water out of my lungs and started to howl with pain. Then the crocodile pushed me into the second death roll.

We came up again, and this time right next to me was a big, solid, branch so I grabbed on to it. I hung on grimly, thinking I'd sooner let it tear me apart than go through another death roll.

Then, suddenly, I felt the pressure relax and realised the crocodile had let go. I tried again to jump into the tree. This time it grabbed me around the leg—the upper left thigh, which was badly damaged.

It took me down for a third death roll. Again I thought I was going to die. I just thought it was going to take a long time over it, which seemed worse than having it kill me straight out.

> But a minute later it let me go, again. I gave up on the tree and tried to throw myself at the mud bank. After several tries, I got to the top and stood up and couldn't believe it; I was still alive.
>
> It was an incredible rush of elation.

In shock, barely able to crawl through the torrential rain, Plumwood struggled toward the ranger's station. Constantly blacking out, it was hours before the rain stopped and the ranger could hear her calls for help. Thirteen hours later she was finally admitted to the intensive care ward of the Darwin Hospital. It was months before she could leave.

The Australian freshwater crocodile can bite, but it doesn't kill. However, it is never, ever safe to be around the saltwater crocodile. Despite the widespread knowledge of the danger, and warning signs designed to dissuade tourists from entering risky watering places, attacks happen and we see the gory images of the aftermath on the television news. The debate inevitably follows as to whether the guilty crocodile should be destroyed. Is it a danger to all humans now that it has tasted blood? Or is it merely a wild animal defending its territory and obeying its instincts? When the victim is someone swimming at night having drunk heavily beforehand, it is hard to be sympathetic to the human who is making free with the crocodile's territory. Crocodile-infested waters are always dangerous. Whether you consider crocodiles to be acting through aggression or in defence of their territories, the outcome is the same.

One of Australia's foremost experts on crocodiles, with decades of close contact with them, is Dr Grahame Webb. Interviewed on the Discovery Channel's program *The Ultimate Guide: Crocodiles*, he explained that attacks on humans are just classic feeding attacks. The crocodile can see some movement or sense some splashing from sound carried through the water. The first thing the crocodile will do is locate the source of the disturbance. It will turn its head and face the source. It doesn't matter if the source is on the edge of the water, or 50 or 100 metres away. The crocodile can dive, move silently underwater and suddenly appear about a metre from its target. Webb told the interviewer:

> I've had it happen to me. I'll tell you, it's quite frightening, you know, because all you see is this great yellow mouth with all these teeth . . . and it's coming up at you and you're sitting up there facing it. You know, it's a pretty sobering experience.
>
> We have a lot of sharks in Australia, too, but you can swim in areas where there are sharks without a problem really. Crocodiles are different. If you wanted to commit suicide you'd just go down to the Adelaide River on the edge of Darwin and go swimming. And there's a 100 per cent chance you're not going to make it.

Webb goes on to explain that most people, especially the locals, are well-educated about where the particular danger areas are and simply don't swim there. And Webb should know. In the course of his research activities, he became over-confident about approaching the normally cautious crocodiles.

As Webb relates in his book, *Australian Crocodiles: A natural history*, he and two colleagues were searching for a tagged male saltwater crocodile which was part of their study in the Northern Territory's Tomkinson River in Arnhem Land. It was on 11 April 1976 when the crocodile had been tracked through the mangroves, thanks to the radio transmitter attached to its tag. The research team wanted to inspect the radio transmitter. Shinning along a mangrove trunk a metre and half above the river, they thrashed the water with a stick to attract the crocodile, something they later realised was not a good idea. The crocodile turned, looked, submerged and appeared beneath them. Mouth open, it oriented itself and leapt at the nearest man. A fork in the trunk broke his attack. Webb and his colleagues never again downplayed the risks of tracking crocodiles.

Some individual crocodiles gain national notoriety. The most famous in Australia, 'Sweetheart', hated outboard motors on his peaceful bit of river. Despite his reputation, Sweetheart did not harm a single human. It was motor boats he hated. Sweetheart lived in what became known as Sweet's Lagoon, in the Finniss River system, a popular fishing spot just south of Darwin. This calm, short branch of the river is about 9 kilometres in length and can reach up to 100 metres across in the wet season.

The first attack occurred in 1974. One night a boat containing three people fishing became the focus of the large saltwater crocodile. Fishing for barramundi on an oppressively hot and stormy summer night, the party of three could see the crocodile's head in the flashes of lightning. Grabbing the motor, Sweetheart shook the boat violently. Dulcie Pattenden was thrown out. When she had clambered back in, her companions started the engine and Sweetheart attacked the motor again. The propeller blades were crushed and the boat swamped with water.

Sweetheart turned and swam away. Three very frightened people were astounded at their luck. The owner of the boat, former crocodile hunter Boyne Litchfield, had once witnessed a fatal attack, so he fully appreciated that he had survived a very dangerous experience. However, it didn't stop him coming back to fish for barramundi in Sweet's Lagoon. Again the huge crocodile objected to his motor, grabbing it and shaking the boat, before puncturing the hull with a second attack.

In 1976 Sweetheart attacked again, damaging a boat's aluminium hull and engine cowling. The same year, a fishing boat containing two adults and two children was lifted from the water and turned in a half circle by the angry animal. This was the first daylight attack, and the boat's occupants had a frighteningly clear view of the large head which was close enough to touch. A moored boat was the next to be damaged—the motor and hull bearing the teeth marks of the attacker. Then a dinghy was sunk leaving its two fishermen in the water. Sweetheart took no notice of them and they fled to safety. Sweetheart continued taking his revenge on the motor boat. Further boats were sunk, upturned or shaken and occupants sent scrambling to shore in fear for their lives. Equipment was lost in the lagoon, but no-one dived in to retrieve it, even though Sweetheart never attacked people. Swimmers in his lagoon were never touched. He didn't want food or revenge on the people. He just hated those motors.

Hugh Edwards, in his book *Crocodile Attack in Australia,* tells of reports in the British press where Sweetheart was described as '300 years old and 136 stone', his stomach bursting with gruesome human remains and bits of motor boats. None of this was true, but it served to increase his fame. At just over 5 metres, he was a normal, peace-loving crocodile who took a violent dislike to boats with motors.

The public fear of a fatality forced David Lindner, a senior ranger with the then Territory Parks and Wildlife Commission, to set out to trap or kill the animal. A man versus beast competition ensued. Lindner wanted to relocate Sweetheart, but was instructed to destroy him if that could not be achieved. No-one considered making his lagoon a protected location. Nor did the fact he had never, despite numerous opportunities, touched a human, repeal the order to hunt. Despite the fact that the Northern Territory had legislation in place protecting saltwater crocodiles, the rights of human fishermen to protect themselves and their property came before Sweetheart's right to his territory.

Sweetheart ignored the baits concealing painful hooks. He swam parallel to the nets set to catch him. He ignored a trap baited with a smaller, dead crocodile. A dead dingo was placed as bait. Sweetheart came at dawn and took the dingo. The sniper waiting in the branches of a nearby tree missed his target.

Calls came from people such as Stefan Sebasten, who ran a tourist safari company, to leave the crocodile in peace. People were provoking him, he said. More common, however, was the call for Sweetheart to be killed. On 18 September 1978 the *Northern Territory News* headed its report on the hunt with 'Giant Crocodile Scare' and the subheading, 'We Will Be That Bait'. Many residents in the Northern Territory had only reluctantly accepted the crocodile protection laws because the Northern Territory Parks and Wildlife Commission had guaranteed that any dangerous crocodile would be relocated.

By 1979 the local, national and international press newspapers and television had created a crocodilian megastar. Lindner was struggling against his respect for the giant animal and his instructions to trap or shoot it. However he knew that if there was a fatal attack, the backlash against the Wildlife Commission would threaten their efforts to protect the crocodiles across the whole top end of Australia. One motor-hating crocodile had to be sacrificed to the greater good. In July of that year Lindner and a Territory policeman went out in a boat with an outboard motor on Sweet's Lagoon, armed with guns. Sweetheart ignored them at first. They stopped and started the motor, reversed the boat—anything to provoke the crocodile into attack. Eventually he responded. In an instant, he had surfaced, grabbed the motor, shaken the boat with its hunters aboard, and then disappeared. They merely glimpsed him. Lindner tried again, but only had a further failure to record. Sweetheart tossed them about in the boat and was gone before they could fire. Surfacing 50 metres from the boat, the animal glanced back at them and then disappeared. Silence.

The safari operators were complaining that business was suffering. Tourists were less keen on renting out small boats to fish in the lagoon. Lindner renewed his efforts. In his next attempt to trap Sweetheart Lindner used a dead dingo, a favourite food of crocodiles, and Sweetheart was finally snared. Trussed up in ropes, he began to struggle. Hoping to prevent a fatal build up of lactic acid in his respected adversary, Lindner anaesthetised him. When the tranquilliser took effect, they set off up river, towing Sweetheart behind the dinghy. At this point Lindner was hoping to relocate Sweetheart to a crocodile farm to live out his life in fame and comfort, away from outboard motors. However, the steel cable attached to the headrope caught on a snag in the middle of the river. Sweetheart's head dropped, and the tranquillised crocodile took water into his lungs. He drowned and they winched a dead crocodile out of the river that day. Sweetheart's body is now on show in the Northern Territory Museum at Darwin.

The numbers of saltwater crocodiles in the Northern Territory have grown since protective legislation was introduced in 1971. From about 5000 back then, there are at least

Adam Britton coordinating a more successful relocation of an Australian saltwater crocodile from the wild to Darwin's Crocodylus Park. (Courtesy Adam Britton)

70 000 now. Such an increase in numbers means increased attacks. The victims are often overseas tourists, but this does not stop them coming. In fact, whenever a fatal attack occurs, it makes world news and it seems there is a sudden increase in tourists as a result. Research from Charles Darwin University shows a strong correlation between tourist bookings, especially from Europe, and attacks on tourists. The rough, tough image of the north of Australia is compelling. As researcher Pascal Trembaly says, 'It's free publicity. The NT gets in the news. Bookings increase.'

In *Crocodile Attack in Australia,* Hugh Edwards recounts many stories of attacks in gruesome detail. One young American woman who came to Australia in 1986 had been fascinated by the film *Crocodile Dundee*. On 29 March 1987

Ginger Faye Meadows took a speedboat excursion up a remote Western Australian river. Driving the speedboat was Bruce Fitzpatrick, captain of a 33-metre aluminium yacht, the *Lady G*, on its way from Fremantle, Western Australia, to Brisbane. The speedboat's other passengers were two of the *Lady G*'s female crew members and a male engineer. A twenty-four-year-old former model from Aspen, Colorado, Meadows was hitching a ride on the *Lady G*.

The King's Cascades on the Prince Regent River, Western Australia, are situated in magnificent country. Tourist brochures showed people swimming there. There were no warning signs. The large pool of water beneath the Cascades was a permanent water source for wallabies, wild pigs and other wildlife, attracting an endless supply of fresh meat for its resident crocodiles. Having explored the falls, the party split into two. Meadows and one of the crew members, Jane Burchett, returned to the boat and then swam back to shore to investigate the other side of the cliffs. Fitzpatrick and the others could see them from the cliffs above. They also saw the crocodile. Shouting a warning to the young women, the others scrambled back down to the water. The two women stood waist-deep in water on a ledge against a cliff. There was nowhere for them to go. The crocodile was right in front of them. Burchett threw her shoe at it, and decided to stay put. Meadows decided to swim to a dry bank, 25 metres away.

Pausing only momentarily, the crocodile surged towards Meadows and attacked. Grabbing her from the side around her upper legs and body, it dragged her beneath the water. Resurfacing for an instant, Meadows reached to the others for help, but there was nothing anyone could do. By now the engineer, Steve Hilton, was back at the boat but he couldn't see the crocodile or its victim. He rescued the terrified Burchett. Turning back to cross the pool, he saw the crocodile surface with Meadows' limp body in his jaws. He accelerated towards the animal, but to no avail. Hilton collected the others from the shore. They took to revving the boat, trying to scare the crocodile, which they finally saw once more with what appeared to be flesh in its mouth. They saw neither woman nor crocodile again, except in their nightmares.

Media attention was instant and worldwide. Debate raged about whether or not the crocodile should be hunted and killed. The victim's estranged husband, Duanne McCauley, arrived in Australia, still hoping that Meadows may somehow be found alive. Crocodile expert Vic Cox was involved in the hunt for Meadows's body. He predicted that the crocodile would have left the remains somewhere to soften in the water, as is their habit. Cox led the search and found the body, exactly as he had predicted, without arms and face down in the water. Cox suggested that the search party wait for the crocodile to return and shoot it, in order to recover a valuable diamond ring, but police and rangers felt the priority was to get the body back to the family. The three-day trip back to Koolan Island with the now decomposing body attracted crocodiles to attack the small launch en route. From there, the body was flown to Broome.

Although Meadows was still clearly recognisable when she was taken from the water, by the time they returned, this was no longer the case. McCauley insisted on viewing the body, which served only to cause him great distress. The body was formally identified through dental records in Perth.

There are many such stories, most of which don't attract quite as much media attention as that of a beautiful young American model taken by a crocodile in the wilds of outback Australia. All leave distraught loved ones and a debate about the rights and risks of knowingly swimming in crocodile-infested waters.

Australia's Aborigines have co-existed with crocodiles for thousands of years. Although, as we saw in the story of Bamboo Charlie and Maudie, there are losses to crocodiles, these are not in the numbers we might expect. In the main, Australian Aborigines have managed to avoid attack when fishing or crossing the many northern rivers. The indigenous peoples who share the crocodiles' habitats know that the crocodile is a cautious beast which waits and watches when seeking food. It does not need to feed daily and will often stalk a potential prey for days or even weeks. Avoiding repetitive behaviour in crocodile territory is a simple, yet effective precaution. Experienced old stockmen, for example, fill their billies at different spots on the river and at different times of day.

Crocodiles attack their prey's weakest spot. Their own weak spot is their protruding eyes. Spears, paddles or strong sticks may either deter the crocodile or be used as a weapon to attack its eyes. Crocodile experts claim crocodiles are wary of people and in most cases they will not attack unless they feel threatened or have a good reason to believe the attack will be successful. They also learn from experience. Having been poked with sticks or hit by spears, they will avoid humans. Knowledge of their behaviour is one way to avoid becoming a crocodile's meal. Avoiding them all together is an even better way!

There is an exaggerated notion of the jungles of Africa where wild beasts roam and any human is lucky to emerge alive. The wild beasts who do kill humans in Africa include lions, leopards, buffalos, hippopotamuses, hyenas, rhinoceroses, elephants and Nile crocodiles. The last are far more abundant than all the other species combined. Where there is water there is potential for crocodiles. Where there is water there is also a much higher chance of human habitation as well.

The Nile crocodile, the most dangerous of all crocodilians, is responsible for a few hundred deaths per year, in a total human population of around 800 million. It's impossible to get accurate numbers of deaths, but for every death it must also be remembered there are many non-fatal attacks which result in loss of limbs or severe lacerations. A human can often escape from a young, small crocodile. It is the large adult crocodiles that are most dangerous. Some accounts of fatal attacks by large Nile crocodiles tell of tribespeople beating the animals with sticks or stones, stabbing them with spears and even ramming poles down their throats to prise the victim free, all to no avail.

Those who rely on the river for water and food are most at risk from the Nile crocodile, but attacks don't just occur when people are fishing, bathing or washing in the shallows. Crocodiles can lunge from the water, striking prey which is at a considerable distance from the water's edge. The animal's powerful tail and hind legs combine to propel it up a steep bank or across the sand at considerable speed. Most attacks occur in the summer months, when crocodiles are defending their nests and the high temperatures provide them with the necessary energy. Although often claimed otherwise, research has shown that making lots of noise or staying together in groups does not deter the crocodiles. In fact sound in the water appears to attract them.

In 1966 professional hunter Karl Luthy witnessed a gruesome Nile crocodile attack in Ethiopia which he documented in detail. Shortly before noon on 13 April, six young Americans from the Peace Corps arrived by plane for a holiday in Gambela. The Baro River runs through the town and the Americans were keen to swim. The local people warned them of the danger. There was a large crocodile in the area, they were told, one which only recently had taken two of the local tribe, a young child and then a woman. These attacks had taken place in broad daylight in the middle of the town with a crowd watching. Luthy also warned the Americans against swimming. They resisted the temptation for a while but then, hearing a splash, Luthy was shocked to see first one, and then the others, dive in and swim to the opposite bank where they played in the shallows, splashing noisily. Luthy was furious at such blatant disregard for the warnings offered by those who knew the river so well. Five of the six swam back to Luthy's side of the river but one, twenty-five-year-old Bill Olsen, stayed on the other side. Luthy could see him standing waist-deep in the water, leaning against the current but otherwise still. Only minutes later, Luthy looked back across the river. There was no-one in the water. There had been no sound, yet Olsen was gone. He would have had no warning of the crocodile's approach and the crocodile took him so swiftly he was unable even to scream. It would have held him under the water until he drowned.

Olsen was never seen alive again, but he was seen. His five companions shouted for him to come back. Luthy looked down the river and saw a crocodile surfacing with a large white object in its jaws. He had no doubt what it was. Ten minutes later, he saw the crocodile again, still with the corpse in its mouth. Olsen's friends refused to believe what Luthy told them he could see, and it was only when he provided binoculars that they accepted the truth.

The commotion brought a crowd, including Luthy's client, Colonel Dow. Although Dow had his rifle with him, Luthy told him not to shoot or the crocodile would disappear downstream. He advised Dow that the crocodile would crawl from the water the next morning to bask in the sun, being so full from its meal. And so it did. The large crocodile was seen on the bank on the opposite side of the river. With his binoculars, Luthy could see pale flesh still hanging from its teeth. There was no doubt this was the killer.

Luthy fired several shots into the crocodile's body as it lay on the bank, but he failed to kill it. The crocodile dived into the water. Many people had taken to the river in various crafts and when the wounded crocodile surfaced it was quickly dispatched. Luthy and a group of men dragged the dead animal onto the bank, where they cut it open. Inside, they found Olsen's legs, complete and still attached at the pelvis. They also found his head, a crushed mass of hair and flesh. The crocodile had abandoned what it could not swallow.

Despite its fearsome reputation, the American alligator is a far less aggressive animal than either the saltwater or the Nile crocodile, but that doesn't make it safe! Florida boasts one of the densest populations of American alligators. The Florida Fish and Wildlife Conservation Commission began keeping records of alligator attacks in 1948. Over 350 attacks have been recorded since then. Until 1973 there were very few attacks and no fatalities, but then people started moving into the Everglades. Between 1973 and the end of 2005 there have been sixteen confirmed fatalities and hundreds of attacks. The Commission's fact sheet on alligators says:

> Alligators are naturally afraid of humans, but they lose that fear when people feed them. At least one of the alligators that caused a human fatality was fed by humans prior to the

The American alligator is naturally far more docile than the Nile and saltwater crocodiles. (Courtesy Damian Kelly)

attack. By tossing food scraps to alligators, people actually teach the reptiles to associate people with food. For that reason, it is illegal to feed wild alligators and crocodiles in Florida.

According to the FWC's wildlife biologists, alligators seldom attack humans for any reason other than food. Alligators may growl and blow and snap their jaws shut to frighten intruders away from their nests, but they tend to avoid fighting humans. Most of the serious alligator attacks recorded in Florida involve reptiles that were seeking food.

Some 'attacks' may be mere accidental collisions. Much the same way as a human investigates things by feeling them with his hands, an alligator investigates things by feeling them with his mouth. When a swimmer bumps into an alligator the reptile has a natural tendency to clamp his jaws down on the swimmer to find out what hit him.

As waterfront living gained popularity in Florida, more and more people moved into what were swamplands. Since 1970 state legislation has protected the alligators, whose numbers have increased. The increased numbers of alligators and people living in close proximity has, not surprisingly, led to an increase in attacks. Alligators have been reported in private swimming pools and on golf courses. Despite official warnings not to do so, people still feed the alligators. As has been observed with brown and grizzly bears, feeding the animals has led to a change in their natural behaviour. They have become less timid and now actively seek food from humans, even investigating rubbish bins.

Despite there being approximately a million alligators in Florida and fifteen million human inhabitants, less than twenty fatal attacks have ever been recorded. Thousands of people use the waterways of Florida daily with no problems. Of course, like many crocodilian species, alligators will take small mammals. As more and more people make their homes on the waterways, more and more pet dogs come with them. Reports of alligators taking dogs, and cats, are becoming more common.

In 1987 the American alligator became Florida's official state reptile. The University of Florida not only conducts research and education programs about the alligator, but proves its claims of the animal's docile nature. At Lake Alice, in the centre of the campus, visitors can see large alligators swimming and basking in the sun. The alligators are not fenced in and are free to roam the area where they breed and live. They may not be fed, and swimming with them is not recommended, but otherwise they do not attack.

Although alligators are found in other states of America, particularly Louisiana, attacks in these states are rare and fatal attacks have not been recorded since formal records were started in the middle of last century.

Most of the peoples of the world who share their local waters with crocodiles and alligators have learned that, if the animals are treated with respect and understanding, along with a bit of commonsense, the risk of attack is small. But they never forget that the risk is real, and nor do those who farm crocodilians.

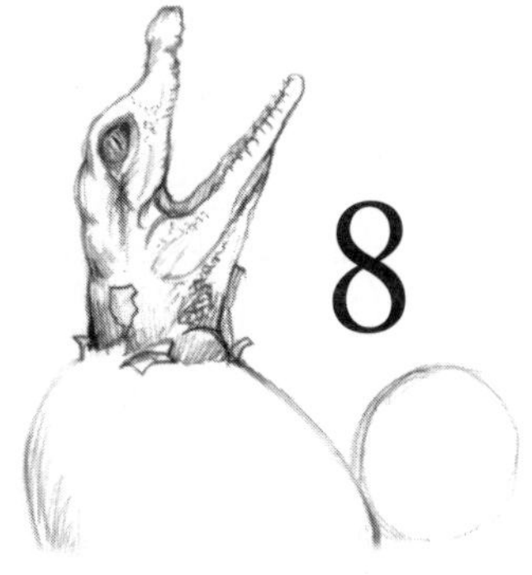

8 FARMING CROCODILES

A young maiden was mated by a male crocodile from the river. She gave birth to many young, so many that she was unable to look after them all. She was not willing to work hard, so she was a poor mother to her many young. She gave some away. She took some to the beach and threw them into the water expecting they would die there. But although the water came from the sea and not from the river, the baby crocodiles did not die. They grew and grew, but they were angry that their mother had abandoned them. Their anger grew so great that they have been a threat to mankind ever since. These are the saltwater crocodiles.

Crocodiles play a huge role in the lives and mythology of the Kikori people of Papua New Guinea. They talk of the two species of the area, the saltwater and the New Guinea crocodile. The creation legend in Chapter 2 tells of a gentle provider, contrasting the New Guinea crocodile with the far more dangerous saltwater crocodile of the legend above.

Australian crocodile farmer John Lever spent years in Papua New Guinea, learning from the Kikori's ability and experience in farming and caring for crocodiles. He remembers the genuine emotion and tears of the people as they shared their myths with him. He believes that the time he spent with the Kikori gave him more than the knowledge and experience he needed to open his own crocodile farm, in 1981 back in Australia—it gave him a genuine respect and reverence for the crocodile.

For many poorer communities around the world, crocodiles are an essential source of food and income. It is very hard to convince someone of the need for conservation if you are telling him that he can no longer hunt his only source of income. Government assistance, such as the Philippine Government's Crocodile Farming Institute, provides resources for crocodile farmers. Planned breeding programs are ensuring that the animals can be farmed for their meat and skins while, ideally, at the same time conserving the wild populations.

Some, however, see crocodile farming as exploitation. Steve Irwin, the Australian 'Crocodile Hunter', was open about his 'hatred' for the farming industry in his television show and media comments. Other crocodile experts believe that farming can greatly assist the conservation of some endangered crocodilian species by providing economic incentives to local people, and as a pool of animals for future reintroduction. Dr Adam Britton shared his feelings with me on the topic:

> I had to reconcile the whole 'crocodile farming' and 'sustainable use' issue myself. Given my background, especially being raised in an environment where killing wildlife was viewed as wrong, I had to do a lot of thinking! The dilemma is encapsulated in this story that I occasionally tell people. There's a question at the end, which I think sums up the decision I had to make.
>
> Imagine that you're sitting on one side of a large canyon—you can see the other side, but you can't reach it. You're sitting there with your binoculars, and you can see a ledge. On the ledge sit 99 of the last remaining crocodiles on the planet. They're vulnerable, being so close to the edge, but at least you're happy knowing that they're still around. In fact, you love crocodiles with a passion. It makes you warm and fuzzy inside. Then suddenly, crocodile number 100 starts walking towards the group. He's sauntering along, as only crocodiles can do, so you have a few moments to think. The trouble is, you're pretty sure the ledge is only going to support the weight of 99 crocodiles. If that 100th crocodile joins them, the whole lot might tip over the edge and disappear in the inky blackness, never to be seen again. Would you ever live that down if you didn't try to stop it?! You'd probably jump in after them! There's only one solution,

and it's sitting at your feet—a high-calibre, telescopic rifle with a single bullet.

The question is, even though you have vowed never to kill a crocodile, will you do the only thing that will save the species by taking aim and shooting the approaching 100th crocodile before it reaches the edge? By doing so you'll kill a crocodile, but you'll save the species.

You have to make a decision. Time is ticking . . .

Crocodiles aren't cute and cuddly. Pictures of adorable baby crocs with heartfelt pleas to stop them being hunted will not have much impact on most people. That being said, I now understand why people such as Adam Britton say that crocodiles give them a 'warm and fuzzy' feeling. As I was researching this book, I became more and more drawn to these extraordinary animals, but there came a point at which I had to accept that they also come as steak. I have to say that the idea didn't appeal, but in the interests of research I met a friend and we went to a restaurant to eat crocodile. The restaurant in Melbourne's Chinatown had an old world charm, including imitation marble wallpaper peeling back at the corners. Up the stairs into the red and gold furnished restaurant we went to take our first taste of crocodile meat. With a choice of lemon or ginger as the predominant flavouring we chose 'Crocodile with ginger and spring onions'. A plate of white meat arrived. It looked like fish but had a meatier texture. Accompanied by rice, the meat itself had little flavour, but took up the ginger and onions well. One of the qualities of crocodile meat, I was reliably told, is that it does not dominate a dish, but provides a basis for it. The deed was done.

I decided to trace the probable source of my dinner. In Central Queensland, not far from Rockhampton, a feast was prepared for me at John Lever's Koorana Crocodile Farm. This time I thoroughly enjoyed every mouthful. Crocodile meat, I discovered, can be served as ribs, pies, satay and fillet, and it tastes wonderful in every form.

John Lever, together with his family and staff, oversees the lives of about 3000 saltwater crocodiles. The animals live and breed in open waterways and closed pens, before being killed for their meat and leather. The farm, established over twenty years ago, is open to the public all year round. There is an initial hurdle to establishing a crocodile farm. Animals take five to seven years to mature and so there is no financial return in that time. Koorana is a business, so every aspect of crocodile farming is exploited, from tourists meeting and eating the stock, to the sale of the skins and meat.

Koorana fulfils the IUCN (International Union for the Conservation of Nature and Natural Resources) and CITES (Conservation on International Trade in Endangered Species of Wild Fauna and Flora) criteria for a crocodile breeding farm. Specifically, all animals for slaughter must have been bred on the farm. Koorana does have some saltwater crocodiles that came from the wild. It can cost a good few thousand dollars to collect a crocodile. Air flight and long haul truck

A saltwater crocodile feeding at Koorana. (Courtesy Damian Kelly)

transport are often required, not to mention the time and expertise of a team of crocodile experts. Under CITES regulations, however, the farm may not sell the captured crocodile's products—meat or skin. They can only be used for breeding, or for showing off to tourists.

Despite the number of crocodiles at Koorana, the farm is not just a large herd of anonymous animals. John Lever has a genuine affection and respect for his animals and some have been part of the farm for so long they are more like pets than breeding stock. One of his favourites was old Goorganga who was nearly eighty when he died. Like many of Koorana's current breeding stock, Goorganga came from the wild where he had become a concern in a popular tourist spot.

Rocky was a young male who did not come from the wild but was hatched at Koorana. Growing faster than any of the other hatchlings, he was destined to be the privileged sire of future breeding stock. Rocky was not going to end up as steak in a Melbourne restaurant. They gave him a female but, according to Lever, he 'chewed her up'. They waited for him to mature. Rocky was one smart crocodile. When he wanted more water in his pond, he blocked the overflow pipe with mud. When it was unblocked he expressed his opinion forcibly by blocking it again. In 2001, at twenty years old, he was given another female, the best egg layer on the farm, the mature Mrs Robinson.

Lever couldn't risk putting Mrs Robinson in Rocky's pen, as he didn't want another prize female 'chewed up', so she was put in an adjacent pen. He made a hole in the fence between the pens, large enough for Mrs Robinson to go to Rocky, but not for Rocky to get to her. The decision would be hers. Mrs Robinson liked what she saw, and she joined Rocky in his pen, blew bubbles into his chin, vocalised and rubbed her musk glands. Her intentions were quite clear to Rocky—he received her with no signs of aggression. Like other breeding females, Mrs Robinson cavorted with her male, indulged in the mating rituals, mated and prepared her nest. Lever watched her closely. When she started to become very defensive of her nest Lever knew she would soon lay. She did. As he does often, Lever reflected on how many millions of years this had been happening. As an older female, Mrs Robinson produced all her eggs in a few hours. A younger female may take a few nights, and can exhaust herself. She will also lay a smaller clutch, so older, experienced females are much preferred by farmers.

In the wild, many hatchlings do not make it out of their eggs. The raised nest of mud and vegetation offers some protection against flooding, but many embryos are drowned each year. If the nest is too dry, the embryos will die. Female saltwater crocodiles have been observed splashing their eggs with water from a nearby pond. The wild is full of predators, like monitor lizards and wild pigs, for whom crocodile eggs are a tasty meal. Should the eggs hatch, the hatchling still has only about a 1 per cent chance of reaching maturity. Predators such as turtles, goannas and even other members of their own species will eat young crocodiles.

To be viable, a crocodile farm must have a very high hatching rate, at least 80 per cent. While farmed eggs are subject to fewer dangers than those in the wild, there are still many risks for the crocodile farmer. If the eggs are turned upside down the embryos inside will die. If any of the nests over the huge area of the farm are covered by water in a particularly wet year, the embryos will drown. If it is too dry, the females may not lay at all. Storms stimulate sexual activity, but also lead to agitated crocodiles. Like all farmers, John Lever always has his eye on the weather.

On crocodile farms eggs are not left to hatch in the nest. They are collected and placed in incubators. Collecting eggs from a crocodile's nest is a dangerous procedure. Careful teamwork is essential. The staff at Koorana have to enter large,

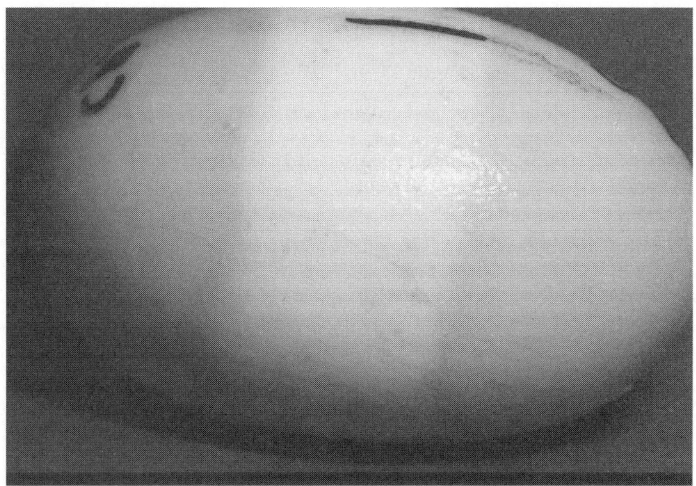

A fertile egg, approximately one month old. (Courtesy Adam Britton)

watery pens and take eggs from nests guarded by defensive females, with the males possibly wanting to have a go at them as well. And they can't just grab the eggs and run. Each egg must be carefully marked to indicate which way it was deposited in the nest so it is not inadvertently turned upside down.

Sixty-seven eggs were collected from Mrs Robinson's nest. Some members of the team carefully collected the eggs while others kept Mrs Robinson and Rocky safely at bay. This was a very large clutch. The nests of saltwater crocodiles in the wild usually contain between forty and sixty eggs. Held under torchlight, a light band can be seen in eggs that are fertile. Sixty-six of Mrs Robinson's eggs displayed this band.

Crocodilians have a special trait, one which farmers can exploit. The gender of the hatchling which emerges from the egg can be significantly controlled by the temperature at which the egg is incubated. In the wild, crocodile eggs will produce a clutch of males and females, some perfectly formed, others deformed, some alive and some dead. It almost all depends on temperature. With climate control, it is possible to produce a hatch rate of 100 per cent healthy females. The truly amazing thing is how much difference a degree can make. Development at 30°C or less gives exclusively female hatchlings. At about 31°C you get a mix. At 32°C and above the proportion of male hatchlings increases accordingly although there are exceptions, with some species producing more female hatchlings above 33°C. The rate at which the hatchlings develop also depends almost entirely on temperature, preferably with good air flow and extremely high moisture content, as close to 100 per cent relative humidity as possible. At an incubation temperature of 30°C, it takes around eighty-five days for eggs to hatch. Raise the temperature and it will all happen faster. Reduce it and things take longer. Temperature is crucial in the early days of incubation. If it rises to above 35°C or falls below 28°C some of the hatchlings will be deformed or, more likely, die.

At Koorana the incubators are kept at 32.5°C, a temperature that has been shown to produce 80 per cent males and 20 per cent females. Male hatchlings, survive better and grow faster, producing more meat and bigger skins. Young males tolerate each other well in the crowded conditions they experience from birth. However, as they approach sexual maturity their territorial nature asserts itself. Hence most adult males must have their own pen. This means that most of the males are killed for meat and skin before reaching sexual maturity, and only the essential number of male studs is kept. Females can be penned together.

Koorana covers a large area, large enough for some of the tolerant males to live fairly peaceably in fenced lakes. With about forty females in his enclosure, the gentle (in crocodile terms) Goorganga had tolerated other males in his area, until one year the old crocodile decided that all the females were his. Using his size and dominance, he didn't even allow the younger males into the water to mate with the females. Unfortunately, at almost eighty years old, Goorganga couldn't service all the females himself, so the farm's fertility rate plunged that year. Goorganga had to be moved into his own pen to allow the younger males to do what was necessary to ensure the fertility rate was back to normal the following season.

Moving a large crocodile that doesn't like being caught requires teamwork and experience. Long rods with rope loops were used to circle the snout of the crocodile, that then rolled, struggled and, being Goorganga, escaped. Crocodiles learn from experience, so Goorganga wouldn't be caught easily again. However the farm's breeding program demanded he be caught and the team tried again a few weeks later, this time successfully. It was essential that Goorganga be subdued and tied as quickly as possible. A long struggle and the ensuing exhaustion can kill a crocodile. Crocodiles perform most of their strenuous activity anaerobically—that is, without using up oxygen—and they must rest immediately to repay the oxygen debt.

Goorganga was moved successfully, and settled into his new pen next to the young stud Rocky. One night storms and floods stirred up the crocodiles and, to Lever's horror, he found that Rocky had broken the fence and entered the old favourite's pen. The young male had a gash on one side and a chewed tail, but Lever knew he would recover quickly, thanks to the crocodilian immune system and ability to stem the flow of blood to a bleeding wound. But there was no sign of Goorganga. After hours of waiting, farm staff searched in the mud of his favourite resting hole and found his body. Goorganga had no visible wounds, but the battle had exhausted the old beast so that he could no longer defend himself. In the crocodilian way, the victor drowned the vanquished.

Life on the farm had to go on. Every day fences have to be checked, stock fed and monitored, sick animals treated. Breeding programs have to be planned and the business managed like any other. There's staff training to arrange and a restaurant to run. Tourists come by day, and sometimes by night, when the reflecting eyes of the crocodiles delight the visitors. Educating visitors about the lives of crocodiles, both in the farm and in the wild, is a large part of the Levers's business.

Rocky's offspring hatched from their eggs and, with the rest of that year's hatchlings, they were placed in huge nursery tanks. Some of the hatchlings would have emerged from their shells in front of an appreciative audience of tourists. They are sustained by the nutrition they have stored from the egg until at one week old they get their first feed of minced chicken, with antibiotics and vitamins. Hatchlings in the wild fight for survival, and only a fraction of them will make it. At Koorana every baby crocodile will be fed, cared for and protected in the nursery tanks.

At one year old, the young crocodiles are moved to larger pens. If they are not selected for breeding, they will stay in their pens, where they are fed well and treated for every ailment. At three years old, they will be nearly 2 metres long and ready to be killed. The methods for killing vary, but Australian farms adhere to the guidelines outlined here in the newsletter of the Crocodile Specialist Group (CSG):

> The CSG urges the use of the most advanced methods for humane killing of crocodilians and offers the following guidelines: The CSG recommends that crocodilians be killed by immediate destruction of the brain by either: 1) a properly placed bullet from a firearm of suitable caliber or 2) by a captive bolt firearm or 3) severance of the spinal column followed immediately by pithing by inserting a rod proximally into the brain. These recommendations have been developed in consultation with veterinarians in the CSG who have actively researched this issue.

The meat is packed and frozen to be sent to restaurants. Some stays in Australia, but most goes to Asia and the United

States. The skins are salted and preserved before being sent on for high quality tanning. The smooth belly skins are the most valuable. The back skin is less valuable and is usually used for lower grade, smaller products. Along with the skins of alligators and caimans, they will serve the fashion and curio industries ending up as belts, handbags, wallets, purses, key rings, hats and shoes. As we saw in Chapter 3, all crocodilians have small sensory pits in the scales around their jaws that allow them to track their prey. Only crocodiles have similar sense organs all over their bodies, and this is how a hide can be identified as being from an alligator or a crocodile. If each scale has a small dot or pimple close to its edge, then it is a crocodile's skin. In Africa, the heads and other parts are often sold as curios. While the majority of crocodile trade these days is legal, a small volume of illegal trade still exists, usually across borders with poor enforcement.

Not all crocodiles and alligators are suitable for farming. Cuvier's dwarf caiman might have the thickest skin of all the crocodilians, but it is also the smallest, so it is not a viable stock option. Schneider's dwarf caiman has osteoderms on its belly as well as on its back, so its leather is not valuable. The Australian freshwater crocodile also has osteoderms on its belly so they are far less valuable as farm stock than saltwater crocodiles. So, while some freshwater crocodile skins are now tanned, Australian farms are more often stocked with saltwater crocodiles, despite their dangerous nature.

Crocodile farming is a fairly recent innovation, with the first Australian saltwater crocodile farm opening in 1969, at the Edward River Aboriginal Community in Cape York. John Lever established Koorana in 1981. Crocodile ranches, as distinct from farms, take all their stock from the wild. They raise the animals and process them for their meat and their skins. Some live animals are traded. The Northern Territory has ranches for both saltwater and freshwater crocodiles, established since 1980. This no longer poses the threat of the days of unregulated hunting. Numbers of both species in the wild have been increasing under a strictly enforced Northern Territory Crocodile Management Plan gazetted by the federal government. Research programs inform crocodile farming practice all over the world.

Crocodile farms are increasing in number around the world, from New Guinea and Australia to Asia, Africa and the Americas. The Siamese crocodile is almost extinct in the wild, but very successful captive breeding programs have been established in Cambodia.

In Africa, Zimbabwe established its first two Nile crocodile ranches in 1965. Despite the Nile crocodile's deserved reputation for aggressiveness, collecting eggs in the wild is relatively safe as the females are very wary of humans. A decade later saw the first crocodile farm in Zimbabwe and the number of farms steadily increased. Soon the concept spread to countries right across Africa. The ranching and farming of the Nile crocodile has reduced the hunting of animals in the wild. All countries have benefited from the knowledge gained in farming the crocodile through an increased scientific understanding of the animal and its habits.

A reptile farm project has recently been established in Dhaka, Bangladesh. This will be the country's first crocodile farm that will not depend on taking stock or eggs from the wild. Using sustainable natural resources by breeding is part of a new direction for Bangladesh, which does not have a strong background in renewable farming technologies.

Farming has a real and valuable role to play in the conservation of threatened crocodilian species. Consider the Cuban crocodile, for example, which has a very restricted range and is perilously close to extinction in the wild. The introduced common caiman has overrun the habitat of the Cuban crocodile, which is also under threat from hunters and habitat destruction. Cuban crocodiles will hybridise with other species, even in the wild. The American crocodile's breeding season overlaps with that of the Cuban crocodile, and there are records of them producing hybrid offspring in the wild. Vietnamese crocodile farms, established in the late 1980s, have reported Cuban crocodiles mating with Siamese crocodiles. As these hybrids are fertile, they pose a real danger to the genetic purity of the species. Without farming, there is a danger that the Cuban crocodile will cease to exist.

Farms for the Cuban crocodile were established in the middle of the twentieth century, mainly for the production of skins and meat, but also with some breeding programs. Now that the issue of hybridisation has come to light, farms can avoid the impurity of the genetic stock by operating under CITES regulations. There is now at least one Cuban crocodile farm which has been given CITES approval to start an international trade in skins.

As well as farms and ranches, there are breeding programs that have been established to save crocodilian species under threat of extinction due to habitat loss and indiscriminate hunting. The Siamese crocodile, for example, is almost extinct in the wild, but very successful captive breeding programs have been established in Cambodia. The Chinese alligator is one of the most endangered animals in the world. Their habitat has been converted to farmland to feed the constantly increasing human population. The alligators eat livestock and destroy irrigation channels. Understandably, the local people have no interest in preserving animals that threaten their fragile livelihoods. Now limited to a few hundred in the wild, the Chinese alligator has been bred extensively in captivity in the Anhui Research Centre of Chinese Alligator Reproduction (ARCCAR) in China, plus in smaller programs in Europe and the United States. Americans also farm alligators, and their research into all aspects of alligator husbandry has informed farming practices around the world.

Farming crocodiles will always be challenging, on many levels, but given the lack of crocodilians' 'cuddly' appeal, it may also be the only way to ensure that species survive both in the wild and in captivity.

9 SHOWING THEM OFF

Siti Fatima, the daughter of the Prophet Mohammed, was cared for by a woman called Putri Padang. One day Putri took some clay and moulded it into the shape of an animal. She worked the clay on a sheet of ipih, the sheath of the betel-nut palm. From this came the texture for the creature's underside. Twice Putri tried to make the creature breathe. Twice it crumbled.

Putri, it happened, had just been eating sugar cane, so she placed the segments of the sugar cane as a backbone. She used the peeling of the rind as ribs. Making the eyes of saffron, she gave them a yellow glow. The tail was made of the mid-rib and leaves of a betel-nut frond. Praying to the Almighty that the creature might be brought to life, Putri rejoiced as it started to breathe and move.

For a long time, it was a pet for the Prophet's daughter, but as it grew it became dangerous and aggressive to Putri Padang, who had grown old and feeble. Siti Fatima cursed it saying: 'Thou shalt be the crocodile of the sea, no enjoyment shall be thine, and thou shalt not know lust or desire.' Taking out its teeth, she drove nails into its jaws to close them. These nails still serve the crocodile instead of teeth to this very day.

Crocodiles are wild creatures who have dominated their landscapes for millions of years, yet, as this Malay legend tells, many people around the world try to keep them as pets. In fact they are growing in popularity, especially for their novelty value. Novelty, unfortunately, wears off. Baby common or spectacled caimans are really very cute. It's not too difficult for a pet store owner to sell such an unusual animal, with its large, gold-rimmed eyes and apparently smiling mouth. Like any other baby, though, the caiman grows. Thus two types of owners emerge: those dedicated to ensuring their pet has what it needs to survive and thrive in captivity and those who dump the animal which can now bite—hard. The general conclusion of reptile specialists is that crocodilians do not make good pets and most countries now impose strict regulations on keeping them.

Both the Australian species, the saltwater crocodile and the freshwater crocodile, can be purchased and kept as pets with the correct documentation. State conservation acts cover the regulations for licensing owners to keep protected wildlife as pets. As the saltie is one of the largest and most aggressive of all the crocodilians—even zoological parks and crocodile farms find them a challenge—they are rarely kept as pets. A freshwater crocodile can be purchased for a few hundred dollars, less than a pedigreed puppy or kitten. However, while the animal itself may not be very expensive, keeping it is. A freshwater crocodile will need a large enclosure with water, and the water will need to be filtered. Filtering removes faecal and food deposits as well as limiting the potentially fatal build-up of chemicals such as ammonia. The water needs to be completely changed every week or so.

Crocodilians are strong animals, many of whom can climb, so their enclosures have to be well built. If you don't live in the tropics, the enclosure will need to have its temperature regulated, which will start the bills rising. The crocodilian also has to be fed a variety of food to match its natural diet, starting from insects, crickets and mice for hatchlings, to fish and meat for the adults. They also have a tendency, literally, to bite the hand that feeds them!

Almost all species of crocodiles are available for sale in both the United States and Europe, often via the Internet. To be sold legally, the various international trade restrictions need to be met. The African dwarf crocodile is becoming popular due to its size. Its temperament is less attractive! All crocodilians bite. They are not affectionate creatures and have no history of being companion animals. Dogs and cats have been bred for centuries to favour their companion traits; reptiles have not.

The common caiman is the most popular and widely available crocodilian in the American pet trade. While shy as hatchlings, the common caimans can become quite aggressive adults, especially the males. The Yacaré caiman can catch unsuspecting purchasers off guard—the juveniles and young adults are often very vocal at night. Cuvier's dwarf caiman is a shy and secretive animal, and one of the smallest of the crocodilians. However, as its hide is of no use for tanning, it is not farmed or hunted, so individuals do not become readily available for the pet trade.

The American alligator is also popular as a pet. Limited numbers bred from American farm stock are available. Some are even kept as pets in Europe. They can be bought over the Internet. Baby alligators can be quite appealing although few of their owners consider them quite so adorable as they grow and almost all owners dispose of them when they become too demanding or troublesome.

Dedicated alligator owners, however, have found that they can train their pets, as this is one of the less unruly species of crocodilian. Most crocodilian species can be 'trained' as they are observant and reasonably intelligent animals. Trained does not mean tamed. Alligators and caimans may be less difficult to handle than crocodiles but it is still rare to find a docile one, especially an adult. When the size and biting issues become too problematic, disillusioned pet owners dispose of the problem. One way is to simply abandon the animal. Several feral populations of common caimans have already established themselves in the United States and Cuba.

Some owners are tempted by the belief that crocodilians will only grow to the size of their enclosure. It is true that, if resources are limited, crocodilians in the wild do not reach their full size. Issues of cruelty aside, this is a very different matter to the assumption that keeping them in a small enclosure will solve the size problem.

These fascinating creatures need to be conserved and understood. The appropriateness of private ownership is a vexed question, but zoos and wildlife parks also have their detractors. For them to achieve their aims of educating their visitors and conserving crocodilians in the wild, we must apply ourselves to learning the lessons provided by those on show.

How can we enjoy crocodilians up close and yet in safety? In their own territories, the tropical regions of the world, tours along crocodile-inhabited rivers enable visitors to see the creatures in their natural habitat. Visitors to wildlife parks can see them outdoors, but still with ease and safety. The alligators' ability to tolerate a range of temperatures allows them to thrive in outdoor enclosures. At the Australian Reptile Park, at Gosford in New South Wales, it is too cold for saltwater or freshwater crocodiles to live in the large swamp. So Australia's native crocodiles have to live in a climate-controlled, artificially tropical environment, while the American alligators have free range of the large lake.

Outside their natural range, crocodiles need warm water and warm air. In the Royal Melbourne Zoological Gardens' indoor crocodile enclosure, the water temperature is maintained between 27°C and 31°C with the air temperature between 26°C and 30°C. The temperature range provides the animals with some variety in their environment and there are also specific 'hot spots' where they can bask as they would in the outdoor sun.

How does someone who is passionate about crocodiles reconcile that passion with their role as a zookeeper, with the fact that these large creatures are restricted to small enclosures so far from their natural habitat? With this question in mind, I spent time with Jon Birkett, Keeper-in-Charge of Herpetofauna at the Royal Melbourne Zoological Gardens. With thirty years' experience as a zookeeper of reptiles and amphibians, and an unbridled passion for their conservation, he admitted he struggles with that very question every day of his working life. 'We intelligent humans can justify anything,' he said with a wistful, self-doubting tone. He continued:

> It is important that the average person supports conservation, not only of the wildlife but of the ecosystems. Preservation of species in captivity is only that—preservation. I don't agree with that. True conservation is knowing they still exist naturally in the world. That's *true* conservation.
>
> Preserving close encounters where people can see, hear, smell and sometimes touch wild creatures is the first step to

getting people to really appreciate the value of wild creatures in wild places. I guess if we're doing positive things for these animals, then the animals we look after and care for in zoos are great ambassadors for those in wild places and our job is to give them the best possible life that we can.

I never feel that we are being cruel, but I always feel that we can do better with more resources. In the thirty years I've been doing this as a zookeeper we get better and better, but in my view it's never fast enough.

Jon Birkett was always fascinated by animals. Although very keen on birds as well, it was the reptiles and amphibians—herpetofauna—that totally enthralled him. Thirty years ago, not much was known about them, especially how to look after them in captivity. Secretive and reclusive animals, they were more of a challenge to get to know than birds, so Birkett embarked on a lifelong mission to know more. He says this is typical of other reptile zookeepers he knows.

The Royal Melbourne Zoological Gardens has a breeding group of Australian freshwater crocodiles and two Philippine crocodiles. The freshwater crocodiles were taken into captivity in the 1970s by the Northern Territory Conservation Commission. Discovered in the escarpment area of Arnhem Land, high above the Kakadu flood plains, they were isolated from others of their species and, at first, zoologists thought they had discovered a new, smaller, crocodile species. Excited media stories flashed around the world before genetic testing showed that the

Jon Birkett, Keeper-in-Charge of Herpetofauna (reptiles and amphibians) at the Melbourne Zoo, is pictured here with an Australian freashwater crocodile hatchling. (Courtesy Damian Kelly)

crocodiles were, in fact, *Crocodylus johnstoni*, the Australian freshwater crocodile, but a stunted form, now referred to as the Stony Country form. As Birkett explained to me:

> This population had been geographically isolated for an incredibly long time. No movements up or down the waterfalls in the river system—a genetic severing of the population by the land mass. But when genetic work was done, they were found to be identical, which to my mind stands to reason. Crocodiles are virtually unchanged for tens of millions of years, so changes which do occur occur very slowly and are not that great. It's mind-boggling that these animals are so successful that there is no reason for them to change.

The Royal Melbourne Zoological Gardens' Stony Country form freshwater crocodiles are the only Australian freshwater crocodiles in the Reptile House, so that they will remain a biologically significant group.

The other two crocodiles proudly displayed in the Reptile House are a male and female Philippine crocodile. While the Stony Country form freshwater crocodiles are a social species and can be housed together in a single enclosure, the two Philippine crocodiles have to be separated. The Philippine crocodile is a solitary and reclusive animal. When I visited the Reptile House, the freshwater crocodiles were constantly up near the glass of their enclosure, watching the fascinated stream of people who were watching them.

One of the crowd-shy Philippine crocodiles involved in the special breeding program at the Melbourne Zoo. (Courtesy Damian Kelly)

The Philippine crocodiles were hiding under rock ledges, although one did venture out long enough to be photographed.

Superficially alike, these crocodiles are two different species with distinctly different behaviours and hence different needs. For the various species of crocodile—indeed, for any wild animal—to be kept properly in captivity, zookeepers must be aware of their biology in their natural habitat. As Jon Birkett explained:

> You need to have an understanding of how an animal lives in the wild in order to be able to care for them appropriately in captivity. Animals have evolved to respond to all sorts of environmental pressures—the onset of rains, the onset of low pressure systems, how to survive a cold season, how to

> survive low food, how to survive socially with each other, how to survive predation, to recognise environmental clues to breed and the behavioural clues of males and females. Every species is different. With crocodiles we need to understand their social groupings, especially of the Philippine crocodiles, who are a solitary species.

Birkett regrets that, initially, the Philippine crocodiles were not housed properly, a mistake he attributes to a lack of understanding of their nature. The female and male were put in a single enclosure and a battle ensued. The female 'beat up' the male. 'Our understanding,' he said, 'was as shallow as a puddle in the dry season.' So the Melbourne keepers sought information from field biologists in the Philippines and the two crocodiles now have an enclosure each.

The two Philippine crocodiles on show in Melbourne are not there to amuse visitors. In common with many zoos across the world, the Melbourne zoo's ethos is now linked with a global conservation program which dictates their operation. The zoo does not purchase animals commercially, preferring to trade with other zoos and animal sanctuaries, such as the Silliman University in the Philippines, the source of these two crocodiles. Formal understandings between governments and zoos, such as in this case, protect the animals from exploitation. Birkett is a firm supporter of this ethic. The Philippine crocodiles and their offspring remain the property of the Philippines Government. The zoo provides resources—posters, literature and funds—which are fed back into the source country to increase public awareness of the plight of their endemic species. It is a global conservation action centred on the country which has responsibility for the endemic populations.

With information from the global program, Birkett and his team are able to judge when the female will be receptive to the male. Then the two can be safely introduced into the same pen for breeding.

The Philippine crocodile needs protection urgently. They are so close to extinction in the wild, they may be beyond saving. Once found all over the Philippines, by 1992 there were estimated to be less than 1000 animals in the wild. By 1995 that number had fallen to only a hundred or so in a single population. The natural history and ecology of the Philippine crocodile is far from well understood as little research has been carried out but, as usual, it is a combination of commercial exploitation and severe habitat destruction that has so endangered the species. It is only through long-term, collaborative, captive breeding programs, such as that between Silliman University and the Royal Melbourne Zoological Garden, that the species has a chance of survival.

Across the corridor in the Reptile House 'oohs' and 'ahs' emerge from the crowd around the large tank containing the hatchling freshwater crocodiles. The breeding program is central to the zoo's activities but it isn't always plain sailing, as Birkett explains:

> The Johnston River crocs we've bred many times over the years. But there was a period of about six years when they didn't breed. It was very puzzling. Both females had been laying fertile eggs prior to this and hatching young. Then for five or six years there was no egg laying, let alone fertile eggs. We tried all sorts of environmental manipulations: cooling the water, cooling the air, changing the light—all to no avail.
>
> We even considered getting another male for competition to get the Stone Country male to increase his male hormones and testes size. The same year we started considering all these extremes, both females started laying eggs. To this day, we still don't know if he went off the boil, so to speak; if it was him or the girls.
>
> Since then, the girls each lay four to six eggs in an egg chamber in the sand and cover them over. We usually know because we'll see test holes beforehand. If you miss that they'll let you know soon enough. If you step into their land area they'll clap you out of the enclosure . . . you do a high step dance straight out of there, avoiding those clapping jaws.

Although Birkett has had puncture holes in his boots, he's never been bitten. This way of defending their nests had not been seen in the wild, although it is common behaviour in other crocodilians. It was thought to be unique to the Stony Country form. However, it has now been observed in other freshwater crocodiles in captivity.

The zoo does not regulate the temperature of the eggs, preferring to mimic nature as much as possible. They do not see manipulating the male/female ratio, as the crocodile farms do, as part of their responsibility. They accept the range of male and female hatchlings. However, if conservation measures demanded it, it's a step Birkett would be willing to take.

It isn't essential for their physical wellbeing that the crocodiles be fed live food, but they are. The hatchlings' chicken and mice are dead and chopped, but they are also offered a range of live insects, including grasshoppers, crickets and meal worms. There is also the occasional live, uncoloured, goldfish. The hatchlings have to learn how to catch small invertebrates and fish in the wild, so as far as possible they are given the same experience in captivity. It is not only the animals' physical wellbeing which the zoo is considering, but also their psychological wellbeing. Chasing and catching live prey provides intellectual stimulus, even if the prey is only the grasshoppers bred for the purpose and affectionately referred to by zoo staff as 'the volunteers'. Even the full-grown Philippine crocodiles seem to enjoy this treat. Although Birkett says they are less demanding of stimulus than the primates, the crocodiles do like to rise from their customary stillness for the odd bit of 'hopper chasing'.

Caring for the animals' total wellbeing, engaging in research and sharing information with other zoos takes a special sort of person. Birkett also believes that all zookeepers need to have the 'animal sense' essential to understand the behavioural and physiological signs of their creature's needs. He doesn't always know straightaway who will make a good keeper for the crocodiles, but he knows who will not.

> The ones to avoid are the gung-ho, showman, macho man. They are an accident waiting to happen. More importantly, they give the wrong message about an incredible animal that deserves to be interpreted properly.
>
> The macho keeper generally reinforces all the myths about crocodiles and puts them in a less positive light. The macho show becomes the focus rather than the animal themselves.
>
> They're not an aggressive animal. They won't attack for no reason. They are territorial animals and so are defending their territories. The macho keepers are reinforcing the 'aggression' by using the word 'aggressive'. That doesn't respect an animal which is being defensive.
>
> They are opportunist animals. They are a hunter. They are a predator. That doesn't mean they are being aggressive. Crocodiles are opportunistic gorge feeders.
>
> And we have to save the species using anything we have at our disposal. Zoos and sanctuaries. These animals are buying us time by being safety-net populations. And if that means farming, too, then I agree with it. I don't think we have the will to save the habitat. We pay lip service to it yet we continue to tear down the forests and fill in the wetlands to promote the success of the weed called humans.

Greg Parker, of the Ballarat Wildlife Park in Victoria, told me of a similar love of the animals and fear that crocodiles will disappear from the wild. He too feels strongly that wildlife parks and zoos have a vital role to play in preserving the crocodilians by ensuring that their visitors are made aware of just how fascinating these creatures are.

> There is a huge social revolution going on where people are becoming so removed from the environment that they become less and less aware of just how important animals, such as the crocodile, are in the ecosystem. A croc is like the CEO of an organisation—remove him and the organisation is in shambles. The croc is like that; top of the food chain in his environment. If you remove him you've got trouble.
>
> Cute animals get overprotected, maybe because we are genetically programmed to like animals shaped like our own foetus. That's not the croc. That's the koala. We need to get it into perspective. It's only the attacks which make the headlines. Huge crocodiles are a treasure as precious as a giant mountain ash tree.

Parker went on to describe what he considers the world's perfect predator, designed for the perfect lunge, with jaws which can snap closed with twenty times the pressure of canine jaws. Yet, what impresses Parker most of all is the crocodile's sensitivity to human routine and constant state of awareness. As he says, 'you just can't sneak up on a crocodile.'

Ballarat Wildlife Park has had a large, male saltwater crocodile since it was a juvenile, nearly thirty years ago. Nicknamed 'Gator' by the press, the name has stuck. Seven years ago, during a routine feed, Parker slipped. Gator immediately grabbed him by the foot. Every feed since then, at the same point in the procedure, Parker is aware of Gator's increased alertness, of him waiting for Parker to slip again. Despite this, Parker says that he would be devastated if anything happened to Gator.

Research on caimans by German scientist Ernst Josef Fittkau bears out Parker's view of the crocodilians' importance to their ecosystems. The caimans are the top predators in their Amazon habitats, but fish populations declined when the caiman populations were reduced. Local natives, logically, had expected the opposite to happen, believing they were competing with the caimans for the same fish. Although the causal relationship is still being debated, the effect has been observed on different continents and with different crocodilians. Theories vary from the importance of the nutrient balance in the water to the deepening of waterways to the elimination of predator fish that in turn prey on the fish of choice being sought by the native fishermen. Although the causal relationship is not yet understood, anecdotal evidence indicates that reducing local crocodilian populations also reduces fish populations, such that local fishermen prefer to fish in areas with crocodilians.

The most famous of the crocodile keepers was flamboyant zoo owner Steve Irwin, the 'Crocodile Hunter'. A natural showman who took his love of crocodiles to the world, he 'hunted' them for zoos and to aid conservation. Irwin's father was so fascinated by reptiles that in 1970 he moved his family, including eight-year-old Steve, to Queensland to open a small reptile park at Beerwah on the Sunshine Coast. By the age of nine, Steve Irwin was catching crocodiles with his father in the rivers of northern Queensland. Australia Zoo, as the family business is called, was in turn run by Steve, who never failed to give his father credit for inspiring his work.

There are currently over one hundred crocodiles in the zoo, all caught or bred by a member of the Irwin clan. The zoo boasts a huge range of animals, Australian native and exotic, but it is the crocodiles and their hyperactive handler for which it is most famous.

One segment of Irwin's television show, *The Crocodile Hunter*, not only demonstrates his attitude to the crocodiles, but also his opinion of those who suggest that farming is the solution to conservation. Each year, Australia Zoo provides each of their crocodiles with a whole wild pig carcass from the local abattoir. In a segment titled 'Big Croc, Big Feed' we watch a large saltwater crocodile, Charlie, being fed this treat. Over the images of the crocodile splashing and thrashing, Irwin talks with his legendary enthusiasm:

> I'd never get this close to the water's edge around a wild crocodile because I'd be within strike range, but I know he's got a mouthful of pig. He's bringing it up into the shallow. When

he goes to break it up—we've never seen him do it before. Let's hope he does—he'll pick it up out of the water, sink his teeth into it and then—head shake! Here we go. Whoooo! Oh, that split it open! His teeth are as long and fat as my thumb. Whack! It's off! What do you say? It's awesome!

It's like sharing a territory with dinosaurs. You can see why I get a little dirty on people raising crocs trying to turn them into boots, bags and belts so rich people can wear them around. Oh gosh, I hate that!

This is the crocodile! This is what they're all about! It's really hard to express how much I love 'em. Seriously, if I could kiss him on the lips I would. I really, really would! And he won't return it to me. Not only am I a viable food source, but I'm a threat to his territory. He doesn't want me comin' in here and matin' with his girls. They're good lookin' sheilas and, quite rightly, he would defend 'em. Nice one, Charlie!

Charlie thrashes some more while Irwin enthuses, even when Charlie seems more intent on grabbing Irwin than dismembering his pig. After a warning from an assistant, and acknowledging the crucial role his assistants play in keeping him focused, Irwin concludes: 'If I make a mistake and a croc grabbed me, all the work I've done in my thirty-eight years goes down the tubes. Everyone's gonna say, "We knew a croc'd get 'im". And I can't have that happen!' And it never did. (Steve Irwin was eventually killed by a stingray, in 2006.)

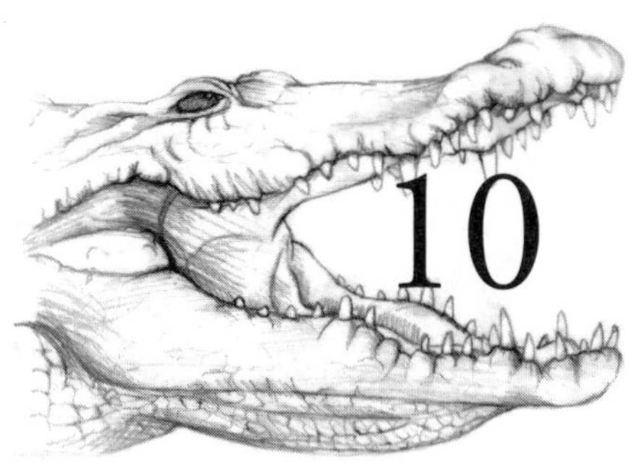

10 CROCODILES IN POPULAR CULTURE

'Peter flung my arm,' he said, wincing, 'to a crocodile that happened to be passing by.'

'I have often,' said Smee, 'noticed your strange dread of crocodiles.'

'Not of crocodiles,' Hook corrected him, 'but of that one crocodile.' He lowered his voice. 'It liked my arm so much, Smee, that it has followed me ever since, from sea to sea and from land to land, licking its lips for the rest of me.'

'In a way,' said Smee, 'it's sort of a compliment.'

'I want no such compliments,' Hook barked petulantly. 'I want Peter Pan, who first gave the brute its taste for me.'

Crocodiles and alligators have been a feature of popular culture for centuries. From folk stories to more recent literature, in advertising and art, their image is invariably one of menace. Jaw-snapping alligators can be found in supporting roles in many B-grade movies where the hero fights off the dangers of the jungle. When a story requires a dangerous creature to emerge from the river or the sea, enter the fearsome crocodile. The crocodile from *Peter Pan and Wendy*, described above by Captain Hook, is one such scary creature.

There are those, however, who work hard, and often successfully, to change the image of the crocodile. Due to the worldwide success of his television show, *The Crocodile Hunter*, Steve Irwin became the most famous of these with his enthusiastic 'Crikey!', the buzzword associated with crocodiles in popular culture. In 1990 Irwin's friend and television producer John Stainton was filming a TV commercial at Australia Zoo when the two men decided to make a documentary, *The Crocodile Hunter.* The one-hour film about Irwin and his animals was so successful when it was shown in 1992 that it spawned over seventy episodes of the television series and many spin-off ventures. In 2002 Irwin entered the movie business, releasing *The Crocodile Hunter: Collision Course*, a mix of his television show and a fictional comedy-thriller about a crocodile swallowing a top secret US satellite beacon.

With his wife, Terri, an American naturalist, Irwin educated and entertained through his television shows and documentaries, Australia Zoo, books and commercial products. In advertising, on the small and the big screen, and in real life at the zoo, Irwin was the most recent contemporary face of the crocodile in popular culture.

Like many children over the past century, my earliest memories of the crocodile came from Rudyard Kipling's wonderful story, 'The Elephant's Child', one of his *Just So Stories.* It tells of the time when the elephant had no trunk, and in particular of one small elephant who was full of ''satiable curtiosity'. After many questions for which his family gave him only beatings, not answers, he was determined to find out what the crocodile had for dinner. Following the advice of the Kolokolo Bird, the little elephant went to 'the banks of the great grey-green, greasy Limpopo River' where he came upon what he thought was a log:

> *But it was really the Crocodile, O Best Beloved, and the Crocodile winked one eye—like this!*
>
> *''Scuse me,' said the Elephant's Child most politely, 'but do you happen to have seen a Crocodile in these promiscuous parts?'*
>
> *Then the Crocodile winked the other eye, and lifted half his tail out of the mud; and the Elephant's Child stepped back most politely, because he did not wish to be spanked again.*
>
> *'Come hither, Little One,' said the Crocodile. 'Why do you ask such things?'*
>
> *''Scuse me,' said the Elephant's Child most politely, 'but*

my father has spanked me, my mother has spanked me, not to mention my tall aunt, the Ostrich, and my tall uncle, the Giraffe, who can kick ever so hard, as well as my broad aunt, the Hippopotamus, and my hairy uncle, the Baboon, and including the Bi-Coloured-Python-Rock-Snake, with the scalesome, flailsome tail, just up the bank, who spanks harder than any of them; and so, if it's quite all the same to you, I don't want to be spanked any more.'

'Come hither, Little One,' said the Crocodile, 'for I am the Crocodile,' and he wept crocodile-tears to show it was quite true.

Then the Elephant's Child grew all breathless, and panted, and kneeled down on the bank and said, 'You are the very person I have been looking for all these long days. Will you please tell me what you have for dinner?'

'Come hither, Little One,' said the Crocodile, 'and I'll whisper.'

Then the Elephant's Child put his head down close to the Crocodile's musky, tusky mouth, and the Crocodile caught him by his little nose, which up to that very week, day, hour, and minute, had been no bigger than a boot, though much more useful.

'I think,' said the Crocodile—and he said it between his teeth, like this—'I think to-day I will begin with Elephant's Child!'

At this, O Best Beloved, the Elephant's Child was much annoyed, and he said, speaking through his nose, like this, 'Led go! You are hurtig be!'

Then the Bi-Coloured-Python-Rock-Snake scuffled down from the bank and said, 'My young friend, if you do not now, immediately and instantly, pull as hard as ever you can, it is my opinion that your acquaintance in the large-pattern leather ulster' (and by this he meant the Crocodile) 'will jerk you into yonder limpid stream before you can say Jack Robinson.'

This is the way Bi-Coloured-Python-Rock-Snakes always talk.

Then the Elephant's Child sat back on his little haunches, and pulled, and pulled, and pulled, and his nose began to stretch. And the Crocodile floundered into the water, making it all creamy with great sweeps of his tail, and he pulled, and pulled, and pulled.

And the Elephant's Child's nose kept on stretching; and the Elephant's Child spread all his little four legs and pulled, and pulled, and pulled, and his nose kept on stretching; and the Crocodile threshed his tail like an oar, and he pulled, and pulled, and pulled, and at each pull the Elephant's Child's nose grew longer and longer—and it hurt him hijjus!

Then the Elephant's Child felt his legs slipping, and he said through his nose, which was now nearly five feet long, 'This is too butch for be!'

Then the Bi-Coloured-Python-Rock-Snake came down from the bank, and knotted himself in a double-clove-hitch round the Elephant's Child's hind legs, and said, 'Rash and inexperienced traveller, we will now seriously devote ourselves to a little high tension, because if we do not, it is my impression that yonder self-propelling man-of-war with the armour-plated upper deck' (and by this, O Best Beloved, he meant the Crocodile), 'will permanently vitiate your future career.'

That is the way all Bi-Coloured-Python-Rock-Snakes always talk.

So he pulled, and the Elephant's Child pulled, and the Crocodile pulled; but the Elephant's Child and the Bi-Coloured-Python-Rock-Snake pulled hardest; and at last the Crocodile let go of the Elephant's Child's nose with a plop that you could hear all up and down the Limpopo.

Then the Elephant's Child sat down most hard and sudden; but first he was careful to say 'Thank you' to the Bi-Coloured-Python-Rock-Snake; and next he was kind to his poor pulled nose, and wrapped it all up in cool banana leaves, and hung it in the great grey-green, greasy Limpopo to cool.

'What are you doing that for?' said the Bi-Coloured-Python-Rock-Snake.

''Scuse me,' said the Elephant's Child, 'but my nose is badly out of shape, and I am waiting for it to shrink.'

'Then you will have to wait a long time,' said the Bi-Coloured-Python-Rock-Snake. 'Some people do not know what is good for them.'

The Elephant's Child sat there for three days waiting for his nose to shrink. But it never grew any shorter, and, besides, it made him squint. For, O Best Beloved, you will see and understand that the Crocodile had pulled it out into a really truly trunk same as all Elephants have to-day.

Rudyard Kipling's rendition of the Elephant's Child having his nose pulled by the Crocodile. 'He is much surprised and astonished and hurt, and he is talking through his nose and saying, "Let go! You are hurtig be!"'

When the literary crocodile is not creating elephant trunks, he is best known for eating the hands of pirates. The crocodile is introduced to many children, and fondly remembered by many adults, for his role in generating the fear in the evil Captain Hook in J.M. Barrie's wonderful *Peter Pan*.

Peter Pan was originally written as a play, and first performed in London in 1904. Peter Pan is a boy who runs away from his home to avoid growing up. Wendy and her two brothers accompany Peter Pan to Neverland where he lives with the Lost Boys. Wendy, along with the boys, is captured by the pirate Captain Hook. They are saved from walking the plank by Peter's bravery. Hook is driven into the wide open jaws of his bitter enemy, the crocodile who had swallowed a ticking clock.

There have been many adaptations of the Peter Pan story for both stage and screen. The first film version was produced in 1924, the silent era, by Paramount Films. Musical versions followed, including those by Jereome Kern in 1924, Leonard Bernstein in 1950 and Jerome Robbins in 1954. In 1953 Disney released the animated version, the latest release being the 2002 DVD version.

Steven Spielberg's 1991 film *Hook* tells the story of a grown-up Peter (played by Robin Williams) lured back to Neverland by Tinker Bell (Julia Roberts) to fight the resurrected Captain Hook (Dustin Hoffman) and to save his children from the pirate's vile grasp. After many battles, good wins over evil, Peter Pan regaining the joy of childhood and defeating the ever nasty Hook. In the final battle, when Hook will not concede and hence, reluctantly, Peter must fight him to the bitter end, it is the huge crocodile which makes the fatal strike. And that is just as it should be.

Crocodiles in film cannot be discussed without reference to the most famous 'crocodile' of the big screen, in this case a hunter who took on the moniker of his adversary. Steve Irwin's 'Crikey!' was preceded by the equally successful 'G'day' of Michael J. 'Crocodile' Dundee, a crocodile hunter who, so the story goes, had his leg bitten off by a crocodile and then managed to survive by crawling for days, alone across the outback. The 1986 Australian film, *Crocodile Dundee,* was written by its star, Paul Hogan. The action moves from the tiny Australian outback town of Walkabout Creek to New York City. The film was a huge international success.

Today's children are being fed a much kinder image of the crocodile than the beasts that seem to spend their entire lives attempting to eat people. Very young children will tell you of the crocodile in *The Koala Brothers*, a British television program produced by the BBC and set in Australia. First aired in 2003, and accompanied by books and toys for preschoolers, it is hugely popular all over the world.

The Koala Brothers, Frank and Buster, are on a mission to help others. In their yellow plane they patrol the Australian outback to look for folks who might need their help. One of the favourite Koala Brother adventures is when they help Archie the little crocodile who has moved in next door. He wants to make friends but nobody comes to his party. The Koala Brothers come to his rescue and Archie becomes a much loved character. As I took the journey of writing this book, my concept of the crocodile changed from that of a beast which ate people to one I would happily have as a neighbour.

Since Benjamin Francis Helpman first saw the crocodiles on the banks of the Adelaide and Victoria rivers nearly two centuries ago, these animals have gone from being a wondrous new sight for the few aboard the *Beagle* to a major tourist attraction right across the north of Australia and in many other parts of the world. The story of the crocodilians tells of a fascinating creature which has spanned the ages and left a fossil record that tells us much about the way all species have evolved. It tells of intriguing animals about which a great deal more is yet to be understood, and of truly exciting creatures that draw us in droves to see them in the wild and in parks and zoos like almost no other animal can.

APPENDIX 1
LIST OF SPECIES AND THEIR CLASSIFICATION

The most widely accepted revision of the Linnean system for crocodilians was undertaken by King and Burke (1997). This resulted in the following classification into twenty-three species (adapted from King and Burke, with common names listed alongside):

CLASS REPTILIA
ORDER CROCODYLIA

Family Crocodylidae (the 'true' crocodiles): fourteen species

Crocodylus acutus (Cuvier, 1807)	American crocodile
Crocodylus cataphractus (Cuvier, 1825)	Slender-snouted crocodile
Crocodylus intermedius (Graves, 1819)	Orinoco crocodile,
Crocodylus johnstoni (Krefft, 1873)	Australian freshwater crocodile
Crocodylus mindorensis (Schmidt, 1935)	Philippine crocodile
Crocodylus moreletii (Bibron & Dumeril, 1851)	Morelet's crocodile

Crocodylus niloticus (Laurenti, 1768)	Nile crocodile
Crocodylus novaeguineae (Schmidt, 1928)	New Guinea crocodile
Crocodylus palustris (Lesson, 1831)	Mugger
Crocodylus porosus (Schneider, 1801)	Saltwater or estuarine crocodile
Crocodylus rhombifer (Cuvier, 1807)	Cuban crocodile
Crocodylus siamensis (Schneider, 1801)	Siamese crocodile
Osteolaemus tetraspis (Cope, 1861)	African dwarf crocodile
Tomistoma schlegelii (Müller, 1838)	Tomistoma

Family Alligatoridae (the alligators and caimans): eight species

Alligator mississippiensis (Daudin, 1801)	American alligator
Alligator sinensis (Fauvel, 1879)	Chinese alligator
Caiman crocodilus (Linnaeus, 1758)	Common caiman
Caiman latirostris (Daudin, 1801)	Broad-nosed caiman
*Caiman yacar*e (Daudin, 1801)	Yacaré caiman
Melanosuchus niger (Spix, 1825)	Black caiman
Paleosuchus palpebrosus (Cuvier, 1807)	Cuvier dwarf caiman
Paleosuchus trigonatus (Schneider, 1801)	Schneider's dwarf caiman

Family gavialidae (the gharial): one species

Gavialis gangeticus (Gmelin, 1789)	Gharial

APPENDIX 2
SALTWATER CROCODILE REPORT BY JOHN EDWARD GRAY TO THE BRITISH MUSEUM

Fam. CROCODILIDÆ

The MUGGAR or GOA

Crocodilus palustris, *Lesson Belanger, Vog.* 305 . . .

Inhab. Victoria River.

Captain Stokes has furnished me with the following note on this species.

	ft.	in.
Length of Alligator	15	0
From base of head to extremity of nose	2	2
Across the base of head	2	0
Length of lower jaw	2	0

Teeth in both jaws vary in size, and are variously disposed, as will be seen in the sketch.

In upper jaw on each side of the maxillary bone	18	2 incisors
In lower jaw	15	2 incisors

The largest teeth are 1½ inches in length. The two lower incisors are stronger and longer than the upper, and project through two holes in front of the upper jaw. Breadth across the animal from one extreme of one fore foot, across the shoulders, to the other side, 5 feet 2 inches.

The fore feet each have five perfect toes, the three inner or first, have long horny nails, slightly curved, the two outer toes have no nails, nor are they webbed. The third and fourth toes are deeply webbed, allowing a wide space between them, which is apparent, even in their passive state. The hind feet are twice the size and breadth of the fore, with four long toes, the two first are webbed as far as the first joint, and the others are strongly webbed to the apex of the last joint; the last or outer toe has no nail.

From the apex of the tail, a central highly notched ridge runs up about midway of it, and there splitting into two branches, passes up on each side of the spine over the back, as far up as the shoulders, gradually diminishing in height to the termination. A central ridge runs down from the nape of the neck, over the spinous processes of the vertebrae, (being firmly attached to them by strong ligaments) as far down as the sacrum, diminishing to its termination likewise.

The eggs are oblong, 3 inches and 3 lines long, and 2 inches 8 lines in diameter.

The skull of this specimen, which was presented to the British Museum by Captain Stokes, has exactly the same form and proportions as that of the crocodiles called Goa and Muggar on the Indian continent, and is quite distinct in the characters from the Egyptian species.

A number of large stones, about the size (the largest) of a man's fist, were found in the stomach.

Messrs. Dumeril and Bib[e]ron deny that any species of crocodile is found in Australia.

NOTES AND SOURCES

1 Encountering the crocodile

- *When the world was still young* (p. 1) This Aboriginal story of Gumangan, the crocodile man, is based on the version in Webb and Manolis (1998). This book, reprinted under various titles, is one of the best resources on crocodilians by two of the most respected experts in Australia.
- Helpman's private journals (p. 2), written on his voyage on the *Beagle*, have been meticulously transcribed by E.M. Christie. The typed transcription is in the archives at the State Library of Victoria. Reading the journals was pure bliss.
- *I had the pleasure of* (p. 4) Helpman (1837–40, p. 60).
- *100 miles more* (p. 4) Helpman (1837–40, p. 78).
- *Weeks found the upper half* (p. 6) Helpman (1837–40, p. 113).
- *There was a Rat of immense size* (p. 6) Helpman (1837–40, p. 179). The transcriber of Helpman's journals notes this was probably a wombat. I tend to agree as a wombat is more likely to stand its ground than other contenders, such as the bandicoot.

- *These islands are a complete store* (p. 6) Helpman (1837–40, p. 200).
- *There are a very great number of Alligators* (pp. 6–7) Helpman (1837–40, p. 262).
- *As the Sun rose* (p. 7) Helpman (1837–40, p. 268).
- *Monday. July, 29th, 1839* (p. 8) Helpman (1837–40, p. 269).
- *Whilst we were coming up* (p. 9) Helpman (1837–40, p. 269).
- *After dinner we again pushed on* (pp. 10–12) Helpman (1837–40, p. 269).
- *About 3.00 p.m. we came to a reach* (pp. 12–13) Helpman (1837–40, pp. 272–3).
- *It has not been named yet* (pp. 14–15) Helpman (1837–40, p. 304).
- *November 3.—Starting early* (pp. 15–17) Stokes (1846, pp. 53–7).
- *This river was discovered* (p. 19) Helpman (1837–40, p. 316).
- *None of my sores will heal* (p. 19) Helpman (1837–40, p. 315).

2 Around the world, in life and legend

- *When Pikuwa was ill* (pp. 21–2) Reed (1993, p. 211)
- *In the beginning* (p. 24). This story was related to me by John Lever of Koorana Crocodile Farm. John lived in New Guinea working with the indigenous people for many years. It was there he fell in love with crocodiles, learned management techniques from the local people, and decided to make them his life's work.

- *There was a small village* (pp. 25–28). Lawrie (1970, pp. 192–4).
- *Once, it is told, Towjatuwa* (pp. 28–31) Terada (1994, p. 135).
- *A young crocodile lived in a swamp* (p. 32) Slightly retold from East Timor Independence Day Committee, (2002).
- *Damura lived with her father* (pp. 35–6) Knappert (1992a).
- *Every Saturday morning* (pp. 37–8) Costes (2005).
- *. . . depictions of creatures with the head* (p. 41) Schumacher (1995).
- *Okuninushi was attending his 80 brothers* (p. 42) Willis (1993, p. 118).
- *Engelbert Kaempfer, told of an encounter* (p. 43) Alderton (1991, p. 16).
- *The monkey would bring* (pp. 45–6) There are many versions of this story as it is one of the most commonly told in the region. Knappert (1992b) and Baumgartner (1994) both retell the story.
- *I will now show what kind* (pp. 47–8) Herodotus in Godley (1981, pp. 355–9).
- *A hunter was being chased* (pp. 50–1) Johnston (1998).
- *There once lived* (pp. 52) Thulamela Local Municipality (2000).
- *The Sun god was distressed* (p. 55) Slightly retold from Alderton (1991, p. 17).
- *It is told of the seven brothers* (pp. 56–8) Parker (2001, pp. 27–33).
- *The gods who created the heavens* (pp. 59–60) These are many versions of this legend, and it occurs in many books, including Leeming (1995, p. 21).

- *Brer Alligator's back used to be* (pp. 62–4) There are many versions of this story, which vary greatly. This version was adapted from Abrahams (1985, pp. 153–8).
- *Once there was a hunter* (pp. 64–6) This legend also exists in many versions and is commonly told. This version was adapted from Burke on the First People website.

3 The crocodilian, in form and function

Consider the chief of beasts (pp. 67–8) New English Bible (1970), Book of Job, (Chapter 40, verses 15–22).

4 Studying the crocodilian

- *She had, the guide informed him later* (p. 93) 'The Purist', Ogden Nash in Patten (1999, p. 236).
- *Mr Krefft has just sent me* (p. 98) Krefft (1873, p. 334).
- *If the old definition still held,* (p. 103) Dr Adam Britton, private correspondence, 31 May 2005.
- *As a young boy I become fascinated* (pp. 104–8) Dr Adam Britton, private correspondence, 2 July 2005.
- *Creationis telluris est gloria Dei* (p. 109) Carolus Linnaeus, Preface to a 'late edition' of *Systema naturae,* quoted in University of California Museum of Paleontology (2000).

5 In search of the ancient

- *So from his shell on Delta's* (pp. 111–12) Erasmus Darwin (2006).

- *Had any human being existed* (pp. 112–13) Owen (1894, Vol. 1, pp. 331–2).
- *When and where did eusuchians first evolve?* (pp. 116–17) Dr Steven Salisbury, private correspondence, 23 May 2005.
- *At this stage, both of the new specimens* (pp. 117–20) Dr Steven Salisbury, private correspondence, 23 May 2005.
- *My zeal and skill at assisting* (pp. 124–6) Owen (1894, Vol. 1, pp. 23–5).
- *The only part of my professional course* (pp. 127–8) Blinderman and Joyce (1998).
- *. . . a sort of cross between a crocodile* (p. 132) Cadbury (2001, p. 316).
- *Those who hold the doctrine of Evolution* (p. 132) Desmond (1994, p. 359).
- *Nearly seventeen years ago* (p. 133) Huxley (1875, p. 423).
- *Hence, if there is any valid* (p. 134) Huxley (1875, p. 429).

6 Hunting the crocodile

- *There are many and various ways* (p. 143) Herodotus in Godley (1981, p. 359).
- *He said his company would pay* (pp. 144–5) Cole (1988, p. 318).
- *It was explained to me by Charlie* (pp. 145–6) Cole (1988, p. 319).
- *Aboriginal hunting may well be responsible* (pp. 147–8) Webb and Manolis (1998, p. 130).
- Data on alligator hunting (pp. 151–2) is taken from a

number of sources, primarily Alderton (1991), Insitute of Food and Agricultural Science (1994) and Ross (1989). Statistics are mostly from US state trade data, which the sources acknowledge are often incomplete and anecdotal. Data that was consistent across sources was included.

- *It's feel good stuff that has no relationship* (p. 159) Murdoch (2004).
- *A landowner can pull the trigger* (p. 159) Murdoch (2004).
- *It is strange there should be a common enemy* (p. 162) quoted in Ross (1989).

7 Crocodile attacks

- *A group of people* (p. 163) Retold from Webb and Manolis (1998, p. 128).
- *I was busy drafting horses* (pp. 166–8) Cole (1988, pp. 352–3).
- *I was in a canoe on a side channel* (pp. 169–71), Plumwood,
- *I've had it happen to me* (p. 172) Webb on *The Ultimate Guide: Crocodiles* (1999).
- *It's free publicity.* (p. 178) Murdoch (2004).
- *In 1966 professional hunter Karl Luthy* (pp. 183–85) Graham and Beard, (1973, pp. 199–201).
- *Alligators are naturally afraid of humans* (pp. 185–7) Florida Fish and Wildlife Conservation Commission (2005).

8 Farming crocodiles

- *A young maiden was mated* (p. 189) This story was related to me by John Lever of Koorana Crocodile Farm.

- *I had to reconcile the whole* (pp. 191–2) Dr Adam Britton, private correspondence, 2 July 2005.
- Information on Koorana Crocodile Farm (pp. 193–201) comes from my visit there and from the ABC documentary *Croc Country* (2002).
- *The CSG urges the use* (p. 201) Ross (1999).

9 Showing them off

- *Siti Fatima, the daughter of* (pp. 207–8) Retold from Corwin (2006).
- (p. 209) An excellent overview of captive crocodilian care is written by Dr Adam Britton and available on the Internet at www.crocodilian.com/crocfaq/
- *It is important that the average person* (pp. 212–13) From an interview with Jon Birkett, Keeper-in-Charge of Herpetofauna, Royal Melbourne Zoological Gardens.
- *This population has been geographically isolated* (p. 215) From an interview with Jon Birkett, Keeper-in-Charge of Herpetofauna, Royal Melbourne Zoological Gardens.
- *You need to have an understanding* (pp. 216–17) From an interview with Jon Birkett, Keeper-in-Charge of Herpetofauna, Royal Melbourne Zoological Gardens.
- *The Johnston River crocs* (p. 219) From an interview with Jon Birkett, Keeper-in-Charge of Herpetofauna, Royal Melbourne Zoological Gardens.

- *The ones to avoid* (p. 221) From an interview with Jon Birkett, Keeper-in-Charge of Herpetofauna, Royal Melbourne Zoological Gardens.
- *There is a huge social revolution* (p. 222) From an interview with Greg Parker, Ballarat Wildlife Park, December 2004.
- *I'd never get this close to the water's edge* (pp. 224–5) Steve Irwin in *The Crocodile Hunter* (2002).

10 Crocodiles in popular culture

- *'Peter flung my arm,' he said* (p. 227) Barrie (2004, pp. 82–3).
- Information about Steve Irwin and Australia Zoo (pp. 228–9) is taken from the *Crocodile Hunter* website, www.crocodilehunter.com.
- *But it was really the Crocodile* (pp. 229–33), Kipling (1978, pp. 53–7).

Appendix 1: List of species and their classification

(pp. 237–8) Revision of Linnean system by King and Burke (1997).

Appendix 2: Saltwater crocodile report by John Edward Gray to the British Museum

- *Fam. CROCODILIDÆ* (pp. 239–41) Stokes (1846, pp. 503–4). The appendix quoted here gives the reports by John Edward Gray of a range of specimens sent back to the British Museum for formal description.

BIBLIOGRAPHY

Abrahams, Roger D. 1985, *African American Folktales: stories from black traditions in the new world*, Pantheon Fairy Tale and Folklore Library, Pantheon, New York.

Alderton, David 1991, *Crocodiles & Alligators of the World*, Blandford Publishing, London.

Asimov, Isaac 1987, *Asimov's New Guide to Science: a revised edition,* Penguin, Harmondsworth, Middlesex.

Australia Zoo 2006, *The Crocodile Hunter* [on-line], www.crocodilehunter.com, 16 February 2006.

Australian Museum 1999, *A Brief History of the Australian Museum* [on-line], www.amonline.net.au/archives/fact01.htm, 7 February 2006.

Barrie, J.M. 2004, *Peter Pan and Wendy*, first published 1911, Walker Books, London.

Baumgartner, Barbara 1994, *Crocodile! Crocodile! Stories Told around the World*, Dorling Kindersley, London.

Behler, John and Deborah 1998, *Alligators and Crocodiles,* Colin Paxter Photography, Moray, Scotland.

Blinderman, Charles and Joyce, David 1998, *The Huxley File* [on-line], Clark University, Worcester, MA, http://aleph0.clarku.edu/huxley, 8 June 2005.

Britton, Adam 2003, *Crocodilian Captive Care F.A.Q.* [on-line], www.crocodilian.com/crocfaq/, 16 June 2005.

Britton, Adam 2005, *Crocodilians: natural history and conservation* [on-line], www.crocodilian.com, 20 January 2006.

Britton, Adam 2006, *Ferocious Crocs* [on-line], http://animal.discovery.com/convergence/safari/crocs/expert/expert.html, 15 January 2006.

Brunvand, Jan Harold 1999, *Too Good To Be True,* W.W. Norton, New York, pp. 182–5.

Bryson, Bill 2003, *A Short History of Nearly Everything,* Doubleday, London.

Burke, Paul, *The Alligator and the Hunter, a Choctaw Legend* [on-line], www.firstpeople.us/FP-Html-Legends/TheAlligatorandtheHunter-Choctaw.html, 10 January 2006.

Burnum Burnum 1988, *Burnum Burnum's Aboriginal Australia: a traveller's guide,* Angus & Robertson, Sydney.

Cadbury, Deborah 2001, *The Dinosaur Hunters: a story of scientific rivalry and the discovery of the prehistoric world,* Fourth Estate, London.

Cary, Henry (trans.) and Carre, Chris (ed. and annotator) 1992, *Herodotus*, The Folio Society, London.

Churchill, Winston Spencer, 1908, *My African Journey!*, Hodder & Stoughton, London.

CITES (Convention on International Trade in Endangered Species of Wild Fauna and Flora) 2006, [on-line], www.cites.org, UNEP, 10 Februrary 2006.

Cogger, H.G., Cameron, E.E. and Cogger, H.M. 1983, *Zoological Catalogue of Australia, Vol.1, Amphibia and Reptilia,* Australian Government Press, Canberra.

Cole, Tom 1988, *Hell West and Crooked*, William Collins, Sydney.

Cooper, J.C. 1992, *Symbolic and Mythological Animals,* The Aquarian, London.

Corwin, Jeff 2006, *Corwin's Carnival of Creatures: estuarine crocodile* [on-line], www.animal.discovery.com/fansites/jeff corwin/carnival/lizard/estuarinecroc.html, 16 Feburary 2006.

Costes, Vic 2005, *The Legend of the Crocodile and the River* [on-line], www.pangasinian.org/2005town/asingan/asingan_name.html#legend, 4 May 2006.

Croc Country 2002, [television program], ABC Natural History Unit and National Geographic Television, Melbourne.

Crocodile Dundee 2001, [DVD], Paramount, Los Angeles.

The Crocodile Hunter, Volume 1: the story behind Steve Irwin 2002, [DVD], Australia Zoo, Beerwah, Qld.

Daley, Robert 1959, *The World Beneath the City*, Lippincott, Philadelphia, pp. 187–9.

Darwin, Erasmus, 2006, *The Botanic Garden*, e-book edn, Project Gutenberg, http://ftp.it.net.au/gutenberg/etext06/8bot110.txt, 10 January 2006.

Desmond, Adrian 1994, *Huxley: the Devil's disciple*, Michael Joseph, London.

Dodd C.H. (ed.) 1970, *The New English Bible with the Apocrypha*, Oxford University Press and Cambridge University Press, Oxford and Cambridge.

East Timor Independence Day Committee 2002, *Legend of East Timor: the crocodile story* [on-line], www.etan.org/timor/croc.htm, 9 January 2006.

Edwards, Hugh 1988, *Crocodile Attack in Australia,* Swan Publishing, Sydney.

Erickson, Gregory M., Lappin, A. Kristopher and Vliet, Kent A. 2003, 'The ontogeny of bite-force performance in American alligator (Alligator mississippiensis)', *Journal of Zoology,* Vol. 260, pp. 317–27.

Faulkner, Raymond O. (trans.) 1989, *The Ancient Egyptian Book of the Dead*, British Museum Publications, London.

Florida Fish and Wildlife Conservation Commission 2005, *Alligator Attacks Fact Sheet* [on-line], www.wildflorida.org/gators, 10 February 2006.

Frazer, Sir James George 1996, *The Golden Bough: a study of magic and religion,* first published 1980, Touchstone, New York.

Godley, A.D. (trans.) 1981, *Herodotus: Book I-II, Loeb Classical Library*, first published 1920, William Heinemann, London.

Graham, Alistair and Beard, Peter 1973, *Eyelids of Morning: the mingled destinies of crocodiles and men,* A & W Visual Library, New York.

Helpman, Benjamin Francis, 1837–40, private journals, transcribed by E.M. Christie, State Library of Victoria, Melbourne.

Holden, Philip 1993, *Crocodile: the Australian story,* Hodder & Stoughton, Sydney.

Hook 1992, [video], Columbia Tristar Home Video, Culver City, CA.

Huxley, T.H., 'Letters and Diary 1851', 9 November 1851, in Charles Blinderman and David Joyce, 1998, *The Huxley File* [online], http://aleph0.clarku.edu/huxley, Clark University; Worcester, MA, 8 June 2005.

Huxley, T.H. 1875, 'On Stagonolepis robertsoni, and on the evolution of the Crocodilia', *Quarterly Journal of the Geological Society of London*, Vol. 31, pp. 423–38.

Huxley, T.H. 1890, *Autobiography*, in Charles Blinderman and David Joyce, 1998, *The Huxley File* [on-line], http://aleph0.clarku.edu/huxley, Clark University, Worcester, MA, 8 June 2005.

Institute of Food and Agricultural Science, University of Florida 1994, *Agrigator* [on-line], http://agrigator.ifas.ufl.edu, 11 February 2006.

Irwin, Steve and Terri 2001, *The Crocodile Hunter: the incredible life and adventures of Steve and Terri Irwin,* Viking, Melbourne.

Johnston, Beverly and Carey 1998, *Paga Crocodiles* [on-line], http://satgeo.zum.de/infoschul/information/Navrongo/johnston/culture.htm, 10 January 2006.

Johnstone, Robert Arthur [nd], *Spinifex and Wattle: reminiscences of pioneering in North Queensland,* originally published in *The Queenslander*, 1903–5.

King, F. Wayne and Russell L. Burke (eds) 1997, *Crocodilian, Tuatara, and Turtle Species of the World: an online taxonomic and geographic reference* [online], http://www.flmnh.ufl.edu/natsci/herpetology/turtcroclist/, Association of Systematics Collections, Washington D.C., 20 August 2006.

Kipling, Rudyard 1978, *Just So Stories: for little children*, first published 1902, Weathervane Books, New York.

Knappert, Jan 1992a, *Pacific Mythology Excerpts: Cinderella and the Crocodile* [on-line], www.oneworldmagazine.org/tales/crocs/cinder.html, 10 January 2006.

Knappert, Jan 1992b, *Pacific Mythology Excerpts: The Gharial and the Monkey* [on-line], www.oneworldmagazine.org/tales/crocs/gharial.html, 10 January 2006.

Knappert, Jan 1995, *Pacific Mythology: an encyclopedia of myth and legend*, Diamond Books, London.

Krefft, G. 1873, 'Remarks on Australian Crocodiles, and description of a new species' in *Proceedings of the Zoological Society of London*, pp. 334–5.

Langley, Ricky L. 2005, 'Alligator Attacks on Humans in the United States', *Wilderness and Environmental Medicine,* Vol. 16, pp. 119–24.

Lawrie, Margaret 1970, *Myths and Legends of Torres Strait,* University of Queensland Press, Brisbane.

Leeming, David and Margaret 1995, *A Dictionary of Creation Myths,* Oxford University Press, Oxford.

Levi, Peter 1985, *A History of Greek Literature,* Penguin, Middlesex.

McGirr, Nicola 2000, *Nature's Connections: an exploration of natural history,* The Natural History Museum, London.

Moyal, Ann 2001, *Platypus: the extraordinary story of how a curious creature baffled the world,* Allen & Unwin, Sydney.

Murdoch, Lindsay 2004, 'When man kills croc, it's bad news; when croc kills man, it's good news', *The Age*, 6 November 2004.

Noonuccal, Oodgeroo 1990, *Legends and Landscapes,* Random House, Sydney.

Owen, Richard (Rev.) 1984, *The Life of Richard Owen,* Vol. 1, John Murray, London.

Owen, Richard (Rev.) 1984, *The Life of Richard Owen,* Vol. 2, John Murray, London.

Parker, Vic 2001, *Traditional Tales from South America,* Belitha Press, London.

Patten, Brian (ed.) 1999, *The Puffin Book of 20th Century Verse*, Penguin, London.

Peach, Bryan 2000, *Crocodile Men: history and adventures of crocodile hunters in Australia,* Universal Enterprises, Cairns.

Penny, Malcolm 1991, *Alligators and Crocodiles,* Crescent Books, New York.

Peter Pan 2002, [DVD], Walt Disney Video, Burbank, California.

Petty, Kate 1998, *Awesome Facts About Crocodiles,* Alladin Books, London.

Peucker, Steve 1997, 'The Crocodile Industry', *The New Rural Industries: a handbook for farmers and investors*, Rural Industries Research & Development Corporation, Canberra.

Reed, A.W. 1967 *Aboriginal Myths, Legends and Fables*, Reed, Sydney.

Ross, Charles A. (ed.) 1989, *Crocodiles and Alligators*, Golden Press, Sydney.

Ross, Perrin 1999, Editorial, *Crocodile Specialist Group Newsletter* [on-line], www.flmnh.ufl.edu/natsci/herpetology/newsletter/news183a.htm, 10 Feburary 2006.

Rue, Leonard Lee III 1994, *Alligators and Crocodiles: a portrait of the animal world*, Magna Books, Leicester.

Schumacher, Mark 1995, Dragon Page: introduction, Onmark Productions, http://www.onmarkproductions.com/html/dragon-taiwan-popup.html, 10 January 2006.

Sloan, Christopher 2002, *SuperCroc and the Origin of Crocodiles,* Scholastic Inc, New York.

Stokes, J. Lort 1846, *Discoveries in Australia: with an account of the coasts and rivers explored and surveyed during the voyage of H.M.S. Beagle, in the years 1837–38–39–40–41–42–43*, T. and W. Boone, London.

Strahan, Ronald 1979, *Rare and Curious Specimens: an illustrated history of the Australian Museum, 1827–1979,* Australian Museum, Sydney.

Stringer, Colin 1986, *The Saga of Sweetheart*, Adventure Publications, Darwin.

Taube, Karl 1993, *Aztec and Maya Myths*, British Museum Press, London.

Taylor, Barbara 2005, *Crocodiles*, Southwater, London.

Terada, Alice M. 1994, *The Magic Crocodile and Other Folktales from Indonesia*, University of Hawaii Press, Honolulu.

The Ultimate Guide: Crocodiles 1999, [video], Discovery Communications, Silver Spring, MD.

Thulamela Local Municipality 2000, *The History of VhaVenda* [on-line], http://thulamela.limpopo.gov.za/welcome/intro duction/ history.htm, 7 February 2006.

University of California Museum of Paleontology 2000, *Carl Linnaeus (1707–1778)* [on-line], University of California, http://www.ucmp.berkeley.edu/history/linnaeus.html, 10 January 2006.

Warren, Brian R. 2001, *A Synopsis of Caiman Taxonomy* [on-line], www.flmnh.ufl.edu/natsci/herpetology/brittoncrocs/cbd-evo–1.htm, 9 February 2006.

Webb, Grahame and Manolis, Charlie 1988, *Australian Saltwater Crocodiles*, G. Webb Pty Ltd, Winnellie, NT.

Webb, Grahame and Manolis, Charlie 1998, *Crocodiles of Australia: a natural history*, Reed New Holland, Sydney.

White, Michael 2002, *Rivals: conflict as the fuel of science*, Vintage, London.

Whitley, G.P. 1958, 'The life and work of Gerard Krefft', *Proceedings of the Royal Zoological Society of New South Wales*, pp. 21–34.

Willis, Roy (ed.) 1993, *World Mythology: the illustrated guide*, Reader's Digest Press, Sydney.

INDEX